PRAISE FOR *THE FUTURE OF FEELING*

"Kaitlin Ugolik Phillips's *The Future of Feeling* is an accessible and compelling examination of what we know and think we know about empathy, along with the complex relationships between empathy, technology, and humanity. *The Future of Feeling* is a must-read for anyone interested in the role of empathy in the workplace, in health care, and in our day-to-day lives. Phillips's thorough research and her commitment to considering each aspect of empathy from as many angles as possible make this an informative and resonant read."

—Bailey Poland, author of *Haters: Harassment, Abuse, and Violence Online*

THE FUTURE
of FEELING

THE FUTURE

of FEELING

Building Empathy

in a Tech-Obsessed World

KAITLIN UGOLIK PHILLIPS

Little
a

No part of this book may be reproduced, or stored in a retrieval system, or transmitted in any form or by any means, electronic, mechanical, photocopying, recording, or otherwise, without express written permission of the publisher.

Published by Little A, New York

www.apub.com

Amazon, the Amazon logo, and Little A are trademarks of Amazon.com, Inc., or its affiliates.

ISBN-13: 9781542041843 (hardcover)
ISBN-10: 1542041848 (hardcover)

ISBN-13: 9781542041850 (paperback)
ISBN-10: 1542041856 (paperback)

Cover design by Pete Garceau

Printed in the United States of America

First edition

For Bob, who handed down her love of writing, though sadly not her penmanship; and the late, great June, who taught me not to take myself too seriously—a lesson I hope will sink in one day.

And for Max, Franco, Joey, and Aspen, who I hope with all my heart will grow up in—and contribute to—a more empathic world.

Contents

Author's Note   xi

Introduction   1

Chapter 1: Talking to Each Other   19

Chapter 2: Teaching Them Young   41

Chapter 3: VR: The Empathy Machine   61

Chapter 4: Feeling the News   83

Chapter 5: Empathy at Work   99

Chapter 6: For Your Health   115

Chapter 7: Best Bot Friends   139

Chapter 8: A More Empathic Valley   163

Epilogue: What's Next   185

Acknowledgments   191

Bibliography   193

About the Author   219

AUTHOR'S NOTE

One afternoon in 2014 I was sitting at my desk, reading a court document. I worked at a legal-news website in a stylish, open office in Manhattan. Even our cubicles were hip, made of tall, high-quality frosted plastic instead of fabric-covered panels. I loved my job. Every legal document told a story, and my task was to clear away the jargon and make those narratives shine. But I was also a millennial cooped up in an office eight hours a day with unlimited internet access . . . so I sometimes took advantage of those high cubicle walls and logged in to Facebook.

It was a wild time to be on social media. Young people who had essentially grown up on the internet (myself included) were coming into our own, growing more socially active and performative. Some attended protests and rallies or joined grassroots political organizations, just like their parents had done in college and young adulthood. Now there was a new place to gather, a new forum for talking about the issues we cared about most. Social networks like Facebook and the microblogging platforms Twitter and Tumblr created outlets for expression and instant validation that hadn't existed before. This was true whether we were posting pictures of our cats, links to music videos, or political soliloquies. Many of us had smartphones in our hands and high-speed internet at our desks; of course we participated.

On this particular day my news feed was full of stories about Michael Brown, a black eighteen-year-old who had been killed by a white police officer in Ferguson, Missouri. The story had been gaining momentum for more than a week as confusion mounted over what had actually happened—had Brown stolen something from a convenience store? Had he charged at the police officer, or had he put his hands up in surrender? How many shots had been fired? Which one killed Brown? And how could all of this have happened in just ninety seconds? Meanwhile, unrest grew in the town of Ferguson, whose mostly black residents felt that white officers like the one who killed Brown did not respect or protect their community but instead profiled and abused them. This was one of the sparks that ignited the Black Lives Matter movement against police brutality, which would grow into a nationwide campaign, both online and in the streets.

From my safe desk in New York, I scrolled through story after story, trying to understand both the situation and the responses to it. Regardless of what Brown may or may not have done, it was heartbreaking to me that he'd been killed, and I thought his family deserved a just investigation. I didn't expect this to be an unpopular opinion when I posted it to Facebook, where so many of my friends were talking about the same thing. But then came the comments. My heart sped up as I read words from (mostly white) friends and strangers calling Brown a thief and asking, "What did he expect would happen?" Some called him a thug; he was big and intimidating and should have known that would scare a police officer, they said. His community was not doing themselves any favors by protesting in the streets, some argued—in fact, one acquaintance wrote, "They're all trash."

I hadn't expected everyone to agree with me about the entire situation—none of us had all the details. And I wasn't naive enough to expect that no one would respond to Brown's death with derision. I knew that racist stereotypes still thrived throughout the country, and that they were sure to come out in coverage of this incident. But to see it all laid out there in pixels in front of me, and to see it come so *quickly*, the comments piling up faster than I could read them, took me aback. Clearly everyone commenting had been thinking about this long enough to know what they wanted to say, but I wondered if any of us—myself included—had really considered how our words would impact one another.

As I sat there at my desk feeling hot and anxious, a private message popped up in the corner of my screen. It was from a guy I hadn't seen since our high-school graduation, eight years before. He was upset about a comment I'd made criticizing the actions of the Ferguson police, in which I wondered whether they should be temporarily disarmed and trained in de-escalation techniques.

I would never call anyone out publicly, so I decided to do it this way, my former classmate's message said. I felt my stomach drop and prepared for an onslaught. He continued:

> I am a police officer. We know each other pretty well since we spent four years together in high school. Until you have ridden with an officer, been through training to be an officer or have put on that badge and answered calls as an officer, YOU HAVE NO RIGHT TO JUDGE US OR OUR ACTIONS. I would be more than happy to let you come ride along with me on a shift one night. If you could see what we deal with every day, see the people that we deal with and the complete lack of any respect most of them have for us and what we are trying to do to keep them safe, you might have a very different view of everything going on in Missouri right now. I am not saying you are wrong. I am not saying those officers' actions are right. I am simply saying that you have very little frame of reference to judge the actions of officers when you have never been in their place.

I would like to be able to say I took some deep breaths, got up, took a walk, and went back to work, maybe even slept on this message before responding. Reading his words now, with some distance, I can see potential openings for compassion and conversation. But at the time, a calm assessment of the situation didn't come naturally. This was Facebook, which felt simultaneously like a yearbook and a battlefield. All I noticed was the anger triggered in me by those capital letters. In a long, quickly dashed-off response, I called him out for using our connection as former classmates as permission to lecture me; I told him I understood it must be stressful to be a cop at the moment and that his job was no doubt difficult, but that his experience in a small town in North Carolina wasn't the same as patrolling in Ferguson, so how much more could he really know about this situation? I said if he wanted me to imagine what it was like to be a cop, he should try to imagine what it was like to be a black man in America who feels threatened by cops, like I was trying to do. I told him, This isn't about you.

He never responded. In fact, according to the Facebook Messenger read-receipt feature, he never even read it.

Years later, this whole exchange makes me cringe. It wasn't about him, but it wasn't about me either. He was right—I had no idea what it was like to work in law enforcement. And I was right—he had no idea what it was like to be a black man. Neither of us did. So what were we even talking about? Anger? Fear? Respect? Entitlement? Empathy?

I wondered for a while what would have happened if I'd responded more calmly and taken him up on his offer for a ride-along. Maybe he would have apologized for using all caps in his message. Maybe we could have both explained our positions more eloquently face to face. I was angry at him for not thinking about my feelings or, apparently, the feelings of the people at the heart of what we were talking about. But I also felt something like jealousy that he could do this—so easily send an all-caps message and then just be done with it, with me, while I ruminated and obsessed indefinitely about the implications.

He was one of the first, but not the last Facebook "friend" to lash out based on something I'd posted. Another former classmate once jumped onto a comment thread about sexism to interject DOWN WITH WOMEN! and then called me a megalomaniac when I responded with annoyance. Another friend, a woman, scolded me for not defending her husband in a debate about the book *Men Are from Mars, Women Are from Venus*. You have a lot of learning to do, she said to me, before blocking me and never speaking to me again.

By this point, I'd had hundreds, maybe thousands, of online interactions. I had first started talking to friends and strangers on the internet via AOL Instant Messenger in the early 2000s. I'd rush home from middle and then high school every day to message people I may or may not have even made eye contact with in the halls. I'll admit I was a bit of a fanatic early adopter, but I wasn't alone—there were always at least a dozen other kids logged on at the same time, and I remember regularly keeping a handful of conversations going at once, well into the night. At the time, these conversations somehow felt *more* intimate to me, not less, than talking face to face. Here I was in a text box with just one other person. I could customize everything, from my font to my manner of speech, and no one else could see or hear what we said to each other. We could be honest and vulnerable, and believe it or not, we sometimes were. I met my now-husband in person but really got to know him via Instant Messenger, where we felt comfortable asking questions and telling stories that might have seemed too awkward face to face.

But as the more modern versions of social media have become obsessive parts of our everyday lives—Facebook and Twitter and Instagram and Tumblr pinging us every time someone likes or comments on one of our posts—their magic of creating bridges is sometimes overpowered by their capacity to help us burn them. As the technology changes and our networks grow wider, we aren't broadcasting our thoughts and feelings just to chosen friends or limited groups of strangers anymore. A whole new category now has access to us: friends of friends of friends, people we know but don't really know. The very act of "friending" can now come with weighty expectations—sometimes for funny content or motivational quotes, other times for emotional support or debate. It doesn't matter anymore if we've only met once at a party or haven't spoken since middle school, or have never even met at all; suddenly we might find ourselves going back and forth in a comment thread about anything from Nickelodeon nostalgia to Black Lives Matter, and we feel entitled to each other's participation in all of it. At the same time, that feeling of safety and vulnerability we had with platforms like Instant Messenger and the early blogging site LiveJournal has all but evaporated. It's hard to feel comfortable enough to access vulnerability or empathy in the quick-fire world today's platforms have created.

Knowing all of this, a lot of critics—some of them former proponents—argue that social media just isn't the place to try to talk about important things. It's true that we can't hear each other's tone, can't see each other's faces. Empathy is certainly harder to muster when you're typing onto a screen instead of looking into someone's eyes.

Online conversations are undoubtedly hard, but that doesn't have to mean they're impossible. For those of us who have lived much of our lives online, giving up on the possibility of empathic connection via technology doesn't feel like a real option.

Of course, we weren't built for this—for clutching small rectangular computers all day and using them to communicate with friends, strangers, and algorithms around the world. But this is how we live now. And, barring some cataclysmic event, we're only going to get more plugged in. Our tech-laden life already goes far beyond social networking—to algorithmic tracking, face recognition, virtual-reality gaming and working, talking to customer-service robots, and buying animatronic toys to entertain children and keep elderly people company. Inventions that felt like science fiction just a few years ago are regular parts of our daily lives today, and there is no reason to expect this trajectory will change anytime soon.

Don't get me wrong: I'm a proponent of the no-phone dinner, and I worry about data protection and online privacy as much as the next millennial. In fact, I will admit that in some ways I'm cynically resigned to a dystopian technological future. (When Instagram shows me an ad for something I was only *thinking* about buying, I am only momentarily freaked out before my attention is diverted elsewhere.) But when it comes to what really makes us human—our ability to understand and communicate with each other through empathy—I don't think we have to settle for dystopia. I think we can adapt. I think we have to.

What started as a fairly selfish search for hope about the future of empathy in a tech-obsessed world turned into a collection of stories about people working to ensure we take both empathy and tech with us into the future. These people answered some of my questions and confirmed some of my fears, but the most hopeful thing they left me with was a sense of agency in what happens next.

INTRODUCTION

Empathy—at its most basic, the ability to imagine the feelings of another—is often described as a salve for divisions in American culture. It can help us understand one another, so the thinking goes that it can make us less quick to anger, more creative, and all-around better people. It often sounds like a panacea.

But empathy is more complicated than that. It means different things to different people. And for all that the word is thrown around, the truth is that, as with many things that happen in the brain, we don't know definitively how it works. Some researchers have pinned empathy to special "mirror" neurons in our brains that start teaching us about others' mental states shortly after we're born. Think of how a baby will start smiling back at you after a few months of life, for example. More recent studies have pointed to a possible empathy gene, suggesting that personality disorders like psychopathy might be triggered by DNA. When the term *empathy* was initially coined in the early 1900s, it was primarily discussed as a state of mind, an act of "feeling into" another person. In recent years it has increasingly come to also be seen as a skill that can—and arguably must—be learned and practiced.

The concept of empathy and various words for it have been with us since ancient Greek times. The word comes from the Greek *empatheia*, which means affection or passion. But that definition doesn't fit with the way we use the word today. Now we see empathy more as an intangible capacity to understand what someone else is feeling.

When researchers started really digging into empathy in the early 1900s, there were two commonly accepted types: instinctive and intellectual. Instinctive empathy involved an uncontrollable emotional reaction to someone else's experience—crying when someone else cries, for example, or blushing with secondhand embarrassment. Intellectual empathy was more distant: recognizing someone else's emotion but not feeling it yourself. These two terms eventually morphed into the two that are most commonly accepted today: cognitive empathy (understanding another person's mental state) and affective empathy (responding emotionally to the other person's mental state—i.e., sharing their feelings). Most experts believe these two types work together, but people often use them interchangeably or say "empathy" when what they really seem to mean is "compassion" or "kindness."

What's the difference? The way I've come to think about it is this: compassion is feeling *for* someone; empathy is feeling *with* them.

Why Empathy?

A common analogy for empathizing is "putting yourself in someone else's shoes." This always makes me think of putting my tiny feet into my dad's big loafers as a kid and clomping around the house. "Look, I'm Daddy!" I'd say. But my dad obviously didn't clomp around in shoes ten sizes too big for him and demand attention for it. This silly memory helps illustrate one of the controversies of empathy: we can't ever *really* know what it's like to be someone else. We can only know what it's like to *imagine* being someone else. So why is empathy prescribed by politicians, technology executives, motivational speakers, and religious leaders to solve all of our social ills? What good does empathy actually do us?

At the most basic level, it helps us connect with other humans. It's foundational for love, child rearing, and caring for other people in all kinds of ways. It also has benefits that are less obviously emotional—researchers have found that empathetic people find more success in business, and that empathy is key for good product development and customer service.

In 2018 a corporate psychological assessment company called PsychTests.com measured the self-reported empathy of more than nine thousand people. Then, a group of researchers compared those scores with the respondents' performance level in thirty-one different abilities. The people who scored higher in empathy also scored much higher in reading body language, conflict-resolution skills, resilience, and standing by their values.

"If there is one emotional intelligence skill that we would recommend developing, it's definitely empathy," Ilona Jerabek, president of PsychTests, said at the time. "Empathetic people are happier, more self-aware, self-motivated, and optimistic. They cope better with stress, assert themselves when it is required, and are comfortable expressing their feelings. There was only one scale where non-empathetic people scored higher: Need for Approval."

Still, not all experts are convinced empathy is worth quite the praise we tend to give it. Paul Bloom, a Yale psychologist and author of the book *Against Empathy*, believes empathy is inherently selfish. It biases us toward the people we can most identify with, and against those we can't, he writes. And when it comes to making a real difference in the world, he argues, it's best to set empathy aside and skip right to compassion. Bloom's research shows that we have a much easier time empathizing with people we already have things in common with, and he builds on existing research about how hard it is to feel true empathy for more than a handful of people at once. One of the most commonly used examples is that of Baby Jessica, an eighteen-month-old child who fell into a well on her aunt's property in 1987 and whose rescue, which took more than fifty hours, was broadcast nonstop on cable TV. It became one of the first viral news sensations. People were rapt by the ordeal, becoming deeply invested in the fates of the girl, her family, and the rescue workers. Baby Jessica became a household name, and many still know who she is to this day. (I was born the year after Jessica fell down the well, but she's always been part of my cultural understanding.) Just to bring the point home, ABC made a movie a couple of years later called *Everybody's Baby: The Rescue of Jessica McClure*.

This reaction tends to be less common with tragedies that affect larger groups of people, a phenomenon sometimes called the "collapse of compassion." Experts think this happens because we automatically regulate our emotional reactions when we expect them to be overwhelming. For instance, when we learn of a genocide or mass famine, we might send some money, but fewer of us will stay tuned to twenty-four-hour cable coverage of the event, because it feels like emotional overload. Some research—Bloom's included—suggests that this reaction can be tempered by the race, religion, or political beliefs of the people affected. If we feel like a person or group is part of our "tribe," we might override that emotional regulation and let the empathy flow.

When it comes to making decisions of national and international importance—as a politician or leader of an NGO might do, for example—some of Bloom's warnings and suggestions may be prudent. If a leader is prone to overempathizing with some citizens and underempathizing with others, many citizens might prefer that leader rely more heavily on another emotion or skill. But I'm not convinced the average person can—or should—distrust or ignore their empathy, and neither are many other experts I've spoken to. In fact, many are worried that we already pay it too little attention.

Empathy in Decline

We obviously don't have self-reported empathy scores from everyone who regularly uses social or immersive technology, but it's hard to deny that there are few better places to see "need for approval" on display than the platforms that keep people coming back for more "likes" and "shares." This is the trait that products like Instagram, Facebook, and Twitter are built to exploit; every little notification and validation is like a small neurological treat, literally releasing dopamine, the "reward" chemical. Social technology is ostensibly about connecting people, but it doesn't often foster the empathy that's needed for real human connection. This problem is hard to quantify, but it's showing up in homes, offices, and classrooms around the country.

Every fifth-grader in Morgan Stumbras's Chicago classroom in 2017 had a cell phone. Actually, many of them had more than one. The devices were disruptive—especially when students used an app called Musical.ly, which allowed them to create and share short music videos starring themselves. "The bane of my existence," Stumbras told me. But it was something else that really bothered her: even though they were constantly sending messages back and forth, none of these kids seemed to know how to talk to one another.

Technically they were communicating all the time—they just weren't really saying anything. Whether it was through Musical.ly, the photo-and-video-sharing app Snapchat, or text messages, they were in constant communication. But Stumbras observed that they cared less about what was said than about how many times they said it. Tools like the "streak" feature in Snapchat prioritize quantity over quality, making a game out of keeping a back-and-forth of messages going as long as possible. Not only is this annoying in the classroom, but Stumbras worries that it causes social skills to atrophy.

When I called her to learn about how she used technology in her classroom to teach "soft" skills like kindness and empathy, we ended up talking more about how her students' tech obsessions had taken over. She told me about one day when she split the class into five groups and assigned each group the simple task of making a poster about a social-emotional concept like respect or integrity. She gave each group an hour to work and a small sheet of talking points to help spark ideas. "All they had to do was color a poster," she said, still exasperated months later. "It's really the most basic of all tasks." But at the end of the exercise, only a handful of groups had finished their projects. In some groups, she said, the students just sat there and stared at each other.

I had a hard time wrapping my mind around this at first. As a millennial, I grew up during a boom in handheld digital toys and games, from the Tamagotchi to the Game Boy Color. We had plenty of things to distract us in school in the late 1990s and early 2000s, even without smartphones. But we still managed to complete group projects with only the typical amount of teenage awkwardness. The technology is different and more ubiquitous now, but could things really have changed that much for eleven-year-olds?

Shortly after my conversation with Stumbras, I visited my sister and her twin toddlers. The presence of technology in their lives hadn't seemed that remarkable to me before—perhaps because it mirrored my own constant connection. But with Stumbras's story fresh in my mind, I was spellbound by the dexterity of my nephews' little fingers on their iPad screens and the way they seamlessly switched among YouTube videos. At barely two years old, they took naturally to this—as naturally as to picking up blocks or asking their mother for juice. They didn't seem to have any problem expressing emotions or communicating (especially with one another—they are twins, after all), but I couldn't help imagining what the world might look like for them in five or ten more years. Or, for that matter, what it might look like for me and the other adults in their lives.

According to the nonprofit Common Sense Media, kids under the age of eight spend about two hours on screens every day, which is not a huge increase from previous years. What has changed is *how* they experience screens—forty-eight minutes of those two hours are reported to be on mobile devices, which is three times more than in 2013. The Centers for Disease Control and Prevention reports that the screen time (mostly mobile) grows exponentially as kids do. Children aged eight to ten spend an average of six hours a day in front of a screen, while those eleven to fourteen spend about nine hours in front of a screen every day.

The average adult spends about ten hours a day "consuming media," most of the time via screens, according to Nielsen. Thanks to Apple's Screen Time feature, I know that I spend an average of four hours per day looking at my phone alone; add to that eight or so hours of screen staring at work and one or two of TV time in the evenings, and I'm well above average for an adult, and even for a millennial (my generation actually looks at our phones less than those aged thirty-five to forty-nine).

There is not yet a clear answer as to how all of this affects our brains, let alone our capacity for empathy. But researchers have made some concerning observations. In 2010, Sara Konrath, then at the University of Michigan, analyzed the answers to seventy-two different empathy-measuring surveys given to fourteen thousand American college students across several decades. She found that as time went on, empathy among young people decreased. College students in 2010 appeared to have 40 percent less empathy than people their age had in 1979. Perspective-taking and empathic concern (acting on empathy) saw the most declines, contributing to the biggest drop in empathy during the period studied. That period—between 2000 and 2010—happened to include the advent of social technology and a boom in immersive online gaming. Konrath's results weren't conclusive proof that tech had stripped young people of empathy—far from it—but they triggered a deluge of clickbait headlines about sociopathic millennials.

One of the most prominent voices sounding the alarm about the connections between technology and a lack of empathy is probably Sherry Turkle, a researcher, writer, and professor at the Massachusetts Institute of Technology. She has compared the impact of technology on our ability to communicate and empathize with one another to environmental destruction, calling it the new "silent spring," in reference to Rachel Carson's movement-sparking 1962 book about the impact of pesticides. Turkle's 2011 book *Alone Together: Why We Expect More from Technology and Less from Each Other* is a veritable tome of research and analysis about how humans—especially children—interact with technology. It covers social media but also Turkle's worries about toy robots and other machines created to augment the human experience. "We build technologies that leave us vulnerable in new ways," she writes.

I read the book only six years after its publication, but many parts of it already seemed quaint. Turkle had been disturbed by the way children seemed to perceive Furbies—the owl-like robotic toys released in 1998 that blinked, flapped, and spoke their own language—as real living beings in many ways, and yet didn't always treat them gently. By the time I read the book, I wasn't sure most kids even knew what a Furby was anymore, or whether they were still available for purchase. (They are, but their popularity has decreased considerably in favor of even more-lifelike toys, like little animals that "hatch" from eggs and fur-covered cats and dogs that move and sound like the real things.)

In other ways, Turkle was prescient. She warned of the philosophical and moral dangers of building robots that are just "alive enough," and what our desire to do so might say about how technology has already warped our sense of humanity.

"Philosophers say that our capacity to put ourselves in the place of the other is essential to being human," she writes. "Perhaps when people lose this ability, robots seem appropriate company because they share this incapacity."

To illustrate this point, Turkle cites a 2004 study that found Americans had become increasingly lonely over the preceding two decades, with nearly a quarter of people saying they had no one in their lives to talk to about important issues. In more recent research, psychologist Sara Konrath has also noted that Americans report being more isolated; the percentage who live alone has nearly doubled in recent years. Young people, Konrath wrote in a 2018 *Psychology Today* column, "may be more socially isolated in recent years, but are paradoxically becoming less lonely." That, she hypothesized, is because they are constantly plugged in to social media, which has been shown to alleviate loneliness in the short term but has uncertain effects in the long term.

Tech Toll

In 2015, researchers in Canada surveyed more than seven hundred fifty students in grades seven through twelve and found that those who used social-networking sites more than two hours a day also self-rated their mental health as poor and had higher levels of psychological distress and suicidal ideation than those who used it less. Rather than conclude that social media was the cause of mental illness, these researchers argued that young people with poor mental health might be using social media more as a coping mechanism. Anecdotal evidence from my own life and the lives of my peers supports this; I've been in Facebook and Instagram communities focused on writing, mental health, and body positivity that served as the only source of human contact and support for some of their participants. Other research has come to similar conclusions. Whether it's healthy or not, kids and adults are spending a large amount of time each day in a semianonymous, highly curated world.

One 2017 study concluded that it's not how much time people spend using social media but *how* they use it that has the most impact on their mental state. The researchers asked 467 students how much time they spent on social media, how important it was to their lives, and how anxious they generally felt, among other questions, including some designed to measure empathy. The study didn't find many troubling associations between social-media use and mental health or empathic ability, until it came to the concept of "vaguebooking."

You may have seen it—someone makes a passive-aggressive or vaguely concerning post on Facebook or another social-media platform without mentioning any names or specific details, leaving commenters to wonder what's up. Some people are so rude, for example, or a photo of a hospital bracelet with no context. The researchers found that young people who made posts like this tended to be lonelier and in some cases even more prone to suicidal ideation.

In 2017, another set of researchers looked at data from more than five thousand people to see how their well-being changed over time as they used Facebook. The results showed that Facebook in particular, more than other social networks, negatively affected people's self-reported sense of mental health.

You may have been affected by the empathy-tempering effects of social technology even if you don't spend much time using it. The ubiquity of smartphones has brought us another new word: *phubbing*, or ignoring the people around you in favor of your phone. A 2018 University of Kent study showed, unsurprisingly, that when people were phubbed in one-on-one situations, they felt worse about their interaction with that person, and they rated the phubber as having lower communication skills and empathy.

In a 2014 interview with the Child Mind Institute, clinical psychologist Catherine Steiner-Adair, author of *The Big Disconnect: Protecting Childhood and Family Relationships in the Digital Age*, likened the communication-processing experience of an isolated-but-not-lonely young person online to that of someone without the capacity to speak. "As a species we are very highly attuned to reading social cues," she said. "There's no question kids are missing out on very critical social skills. In a way, texting and online communicating . . . puts everybody in a nonverbal disabled context, where body language, facial expression, and even the smallest kind of vocal reactions are rendered invisible."

I have felt the toll of this myself as an adult. The starkest example was my former classmate, the current law-enforcement officer, messaging me to stop talking about the killing of Michael Brown in Ferguson, Missouri. Would he have yelled "YOU HAVE NO RIGHT

TO JUDGE US OR OUR ACTIONS" to my face if we'd been talking in person? Would either of us have brought up this issue at all in such close proximity? It seemed like something we might have talked about when we knew each other in high school, but now it felt almost impolite to argue face to face.

He had felt judged by my public post, but I hadn't thought I was judging him. I hadn't thought about him or the other cops I knew at all. I was thinking about the young man who was dead and the millions of others who were afraid for their own lives. At the same time, my former classmate saw something in my posts that I didn't know was there, and it triggered something in him. *How could he not see the real issue here?* I had wondered. It wasn't until much later that I realized he probably wondered the same thing about me. There had been no room for questions or learning in that exchange, for either of us. No space for true vulnerability or even an honest response. I simply felt entitled to post my thoughts in my little corner of Facebook, and he felt entitled (based in part, he said, on the fact that we'd known each other years before) to reprimand me privately. Then, both of our pieces said, it was over. After years of posting and liking and scrolling past things that might have once been IRL (in-real-life) conversations, this felt like a natural progression toward a most unnatural kind of communication.

As I sat staring at the computer screen the day I received that Facebook message, and in the days and weeks that followed, this interaction stayed with me. I began to worry that there was something to the warnings from experts like Turkle. It wasn't just my interaction with my former classmate—I saw similar exchanges happening on social media every day.

My experience online has been nothing compared to what some people go through. Our new social-tech culture has made it seem acceptable to verbally attack "friends" and strangers alike in the most vulgar ways. Women and members of other marginalized groups are often especially vulnerable to these kinds of attacks on the internet, and

I've had my fair share of random trolls calling me names and wishing fates upon me that I won't print here. But get a little bit of notoriety or fame, and your "fair share" of trolling grows exponentially. Franchesca Ramsey, an activist and actress who gained fame from a series of viral YouTube videos, writes about this poignantly in her book *Well, That Escalated Quickly: Memoirs and Mistakes of an Accidental Activist*. She became somewhat used to the vitriol of commenters on her YouTube videos, which tackle tough subjects like racism with humor. But when she started writing for and appearing regularly on *The Nightly Show with Larry Wilmore*, things took a turn. She writes:

> No matter what I did, I couldn't stop the onslaught of harassment and anger that followed every single one of my appearances. All the criticism was funneled through social media, which I was using all the time, during breaks or in the dressing room. I knew I should just ignore the trolls . . . but often the comments were so vicious that I felt I had to defend myself, or I at least wanted the catharsis of having fully explained my position. Though I had great relationships with everyone I worked with, I secretly cried in the bathroom pretty much every day.

But at the same time, Ramsey—like many of the people you will meet in the following pages—freely admits that she owes her career to the social internet and has no plans to leave it.

Platforms like Facebook and Twitter can feel like battlefields where it's hard for us to convince one another to set down our weapons long enough to understand a different experience or perspective. Opportunities to talk *at* each other are so common, and the energy to really listen is so limited, that it can feel like we're spending most of our online time on the defense. Meanwhile, bad news seems worse than ever, and some days it seems like the only way to cope with the sensational headlines and endless tweets and posts about death and destruction around the world is to ignore them. In a world in which we're each increasingly individualistic while also being constantly tethered digitally to others, everything is presented as extreme and binary.

At the time I received the message from my former classmate, it seemed like the evidence was all around me that this new reality was squeezing out empathy.

What's Next

In the grand scheme of things, online scuffles and tech gadgets can seem unimportant. But if being plugged in affects our ability to empathize, there's actually something much deeper at stake than online discomfort. Being able to recognize—if not always fully understand—another person's mind-set or perspective is about more than having civil conversations. Empathy is also key to learning, child rearing, and participating in a human community, both online and off.

My own concerns about the effects of this online life collided with my work as a journalist when I started reporting on health-care technology and got more familiar with the ways our lives are increasingly embedded in the digital world. Algorithms, activity trackers, artificial intelligence, and virtual reality are sometimes advertised as benign, even savior-like, innovations. The Fitbit can help us lose weight, a virtual trip to the beach can help us de-stress, and algorithms tracking our internet activity may even be able to tell if we're depressed or suicidal. But as I learned more, I couldn't help but wonder: If our interpersonal connections are already this frayed by phones and social media, how much worse could it get as tech becomes even more pervasive and we become even more dependent on it? What will happen to empathy in an even more tech-obsessed future?

As it turns out, many in the tech industry—and many hoping to break in—are asking the same questions. Whether because of the ubiquity of tech, the worsening of political divisions, or a recent boom in social-science research, a growing number of people—parents, teachers, journalists, and consumers—are talking and worrying about empathy. Job-hunting websites regularly tout the importance of empathy in setting oneself apart, and business and advertising publications warn that without more of it, companies risk losing customers. In fact, our ability to empathize is often singled out as one of the few human skills that make us more qualified than robots for many jobs that involve communication and collaboration. Popular media is also increasingly tackling the issue head-on. The tech-dystopia series *Black Mirror* has garnered a cult following, each episode showing what life might be like for us and our technology in a near future with just a little more surveillance and a little more dependence on the algorithms all around us. According to the show's creator, Charlie Brooker, each episode is supposed to be about "the way we live now—and the way we might be living in ten minutes' time if we're clumsy."

Picking up on the zeitgeist, tech companies have been increasingly using empathy as a marketing tool, with even the embattled Mark Zuckerberg claiming that Facebook, site of so much division and drama over the past decade in public and private life, can help create empathy because it helps people bond over shared interests. In 2017, Zuckerberg took this effort a step further, inserting a cartoon of himself into video footage of Puerto Rico in an empathy-building virtual-reality experiment. It ended up falling flat; many viewers found it more goofy than empathetic.

Virtual reality (VR), a combination of technologies that allows the user to experience a 360-degree environment, was dubbed "the empathy machine" by filmmaker Chris Milk in a 2015 TED Talk; it has been touted by tech titans and nonprofits alike as a tool with the potential to force even the most hard-hearted to understand and care about people who are different from them. When the United Nations began using VR to transport people to communities in great need around the world, the organization said the number of donations doubled. But VR comes with its own concerns, from motion sickness to manipulation.

We know empathy can't solve all our problems, and Big Tech, though it has sky-high ambitions, certainly can't do it alone either. But can the same technologies that we blame for exacerbating these problems be used to help us fix them? If so, what does that say about us as humans? Empathy is still one of the factors that set us apart from machines and many animals. That sense of not just knowing the facts of someone else's experience but experiencing it in our own way, and following that path to deeper understanding and compassion, is still uniquely ours. It can seem sad to require an assist from technology to harness empathy. But this is exactly the kind of thing that we create technology to do.

While some of us fumble to balance our awkward relationships to machines and each other, there is a growing band of teachers, futurists, engineers, designers, and communicators working to ensure that we take empathy with us into the future. People like Jane McGonigal, who created a game to help kids imagine things that don't exist yet but soon could, like emotion trackers that let you share your feelings in real time. And Natalie Egan, of tech consultancy Translator, who uses virtual reality, chatbots, and apps to improve diversity and inclusion at major corporations. And 360-degree-video documentarian Nonny de la Peña, who has inspired a new type of immersive journalism that puts news consumers into moments they would otherwise only read or hear about.

This work is important now not just because of the speed of technological innovation but because a confluence of problems that are hard to understand, let alone solve, has left many people looking for softer, more compassionate answers.

Building the Future

The most encouraging (and sometimes surprising) thing I've learned through this work has been how natural these ideas seem to young people. I—a millennial in my early thirties—often have to make a conscious effort to connect technological innovations with empathy in my own mind. But to the generation after mine, often called Gen Z or iGen, technology that teaches things like empathy, inclusivity, vulnerability, and emotional problem solving seems like a no-brainer.

Jean Twenge, a psychologist who has been studying generational differences for more than twenty-five years, says members of this younger generation are characterized by their near-complete immersion in technology, mostly through smartphones. Most of them don't remember a time before ubiquitous internet, and a 2017 study of more than five thousand of them found that three-quarters owned an iPhone. Through her work, Twenge has found that each subsequent generation seems to have a tougher and tougher time with communication and happiness. But in her most recent work on iGen, she has seen some hopeful signs. In a widely shared *Atlantic* article titled "Have Smartphones Destroyed a Generation?" the answer seems to be "not necessarily." She wrote that in her conversations with teens (yes, those are possible!), she noticed many of them were cognizant of the connection between their problems with loneliness, anxiety, depression, and interpersonal conflict, and their dependence on technology. They notice when they're being phubbed and sometimes when they're guilty of it themselves. And they seem aware that this isn't the most fulfilling way to live.

How we feel when walking away from any tech experience—VR, games, apps, encounters with algorithms and robots—is necessarily informed by where we come from, our own sense of identity, and the identities of the people who created the experience. The irony of asking us to lean further into technology to help combat its most antisocial effects runs deep and is acknowledged at varying levels by the people creating these worlds for us to inhabit. When I've asked creators and users to address this paradox, they've most often responded with a mixture of humility and hope. Almost no one believes that games, bots, and social media will save us. But few think they will be our downfall either. The most common refrain echoes what Welela Solomon, an eighth-grader making the rounds on the tech-conference circuit in 2018, said when asked about artificial intelligence: Tech is a tool. It does what we tell it to do.

The makers and operators of our current tools have made a lot of mistakes—and some harmful deliberate decisions. The creators of the next generation of tech have an unprecedented opportunity to change the trajectory, and many see empathy as the key.

CHAPTER 1
TALKING TO EACH OTHER

One of the internet's greatest promises is access to conversations with people all around the world—people we may never otherwise meet, in places we may never go. In the beginning it connected scientists, academics, and business leaders across the globe, and then it allowed kids like me to enter anonymous chat rooms and "meet" pen pals in far-flung places. It also opened the door to harassment, abuse, and "catfishing"— creating a fake identity and using it to get attention, extort money, or carry on false romantic relationships. In the 2010s, of course, it's a well-accepted fact that both things are true—talking to people online can sometimes open our minds and allow us to give and receive empathy at levels never before possible, and it can also make us angry, resentful, bitter, hostile, and depressed. While some people thrive on finding connection online, for others the digital world is a place of suffering. One thing is for sure: the internet has been a laboratory for a new form of communication, for better or worse.

The impact can be seen most clearly on social media, where conversations often feel more like games. I first started noticing this around 2014 in the comment sections of news articles and posts in Facebook groups, especially those about controversial topics related to race, feminism, and other social-justice issues. Some people seemed to seek these out just to argue. These debaters would jump into a conversation and demand clarification or well-researched proof, and if their unwitting sparring partner wasn't game, they would run through a list of common accusations ("That's a straw-man argument!"; "You just don't like logic!") and taunt the other person for being "afraid of a little debate." Too often, they would become hostile and abusive, sometimes even creating new accounts to keep bothering an opponent after being blocked.

I've never been averse to the idea of debate on important issues. But a person entering a conversation online—especially with strangers—can't be assumed to be armed with Robert's Rules of Order. In an actual debate—formal or not—both people are usually aware of the stakes and have previously agreed on some rules. On social media, you never know when someone might swoop into a comment thread and demand that everyone else start playing by their rule book. And if you don't comply, they "win."

People like this are often called "trolls." Some of them have one goal: to derail a conversation and turn the attention on themselves. They will start off civil, then purposely change their rules with every response from their target, and they feel they've won if the other person seems angry or upset or shows any emotion.

These are extreme examples of conversation gamification, but it's easy to see in just about every online comment thread that there are numerous people—trolls or not—who start or join conversations with the sole intent of winning. Sometimes a win looks like validation in the form of likes and retweets, more followers, or the satisfaction of being right; sometimes it's about making another person so angry or upset that they fight back for hours or hit the "Block" button. This sounds like a waste of time for everyone involved, but in the thick of these conversations, it can really feel impossible to walk away. I will admit I've been on both sides. The desire to win is infectious, and when it's a topic I'm passionate about—women's rights, for example—it can feel imperative to beat a conversational adversary. It took me longer than I'd like to admit to realize that most of the time on social media, especially with strangers, I wasn't having real debates or even real conversations; more often than not, it was just a game to the other person. Even when the topic was sexual assault or police brutality, I found myself—and saw my friends—regularly sparring with people who were either simply saying outrageous things to get a rise out of us, or who seemed to have no empathy about the situations being discussed but felt entitled to opine on them and, if they could, to "win."

The problem exists among those with good intentions too. Without tone of voice, facial expressions, or any real accountability for what we say, even those of us with the best intentions can have a hard time remembering the humanity of the people on the other side of the keyboard. The former classmate I sparred with on Facebook about police brutality had something real to say to me, but it was clear by the way he presented it that he didn't even want a debate—he simply wanted to pour out his words, screw on the top, and throw the bottle away. That probably felt good for a few minutes. But I know from experience that that feeling likely didn't last. I've won my share of online battles too, and I even saw that conversation as won for a while when he didn't answer. In the trenches of social media, it can feel good in the moment to have pelted your opponent into submission with long, eloquent comments and carefully researched links. But whenever I've had this experience, I've always felt tired, anxious, embarrassed, and still upset about the thing I'd posted about in the first place. I've never changed anyone's mind or convinced them to see things my way in these gamified conversations. I never furthered any cause or helped myself come to peace with awful things in the world. I just raised my blood pressure, lost a few friends, and pissed off some family members.

This dynamic started to become a real problem for me in the lead-up to the 2016 election, when I found myself spending hours each day reading and participating in discussions about politics on social media. I wasn't alone. Dozens of articles have been written about the unique tension of a conversation between someone who supports Donald Trump and someone who does not. I now feel safe saying that almost nothing was gained from these exchanges between strangers, but at the time it felt so urgent. I tried to avoid sparring with people I didn't know, but the online conversations I tried to have with friends and distant family members were even harder. It wasn't just about political differences; looking back, it seems clear that we often got stuck because we were trying to force feelings of empathy onto one another—for the poor white working class, for Mexican immigrants, for people who felt forgotten by past presidents, for people who feared for their future under this one— through a medium that wasn't built for it. At the time, strangers and friends alike seemed baffled as to why they weren't being understood or believed. And the fear of what might happen if the election went one way or the other made everything seem so urgent that there was no time to listen. I found myself constantly thinking about whether it was a fundamental lack of understanding and empathy for one another that had led to the country's massive division and wondering what role gamified conversation had played.

Much has been written about trolling, public shaming, and doxing (publishing someone's private contact information online in an act of aggression or revenge). These issues have been bubbling under the surface for years, but it was the 2016 US presidential election that seemed to really bring them to the fore of the national conversation.

During the campaign, two conversation researchers—Joseph Grenny and David Maxfield, founders of business-consulting firm VitalSmarts and authors of *Crucial Conversations: Tools for Talking When Stakes Are High*—conducted a poll of 1,866 Americans and found that 90 percent of them felt the 2016 election season had been more polarizing than the one in 2012. One-third of respondents said they had been "attacked, insulted, or called names" because of their political views, and one in four said their relationships had suffered. More than a quarter of these troublesome conversations were reported to have happened on social media. Grenny and Maxfield noted that 81 percent of those polled said their solution to all this drama was to simply avoid talking about politics altogether. It wasn't always specific controversial topics that divided these people and their conversational partners—it was support for individual candidates, and how that support was tied to identity. To illustrate, the authors asked people to describe supporters of the candidate they didn't like. These were the top adjectives respondents used on both sides: *angry, uneducated, ignorant, uninformed, racist, white, narrow,* and *blind.*

"With this kind of tainted perspective, it's no wonder we come into a politically oriented conversation itching for a fight," Grenny said at the time.

Other research helps explain what's going on in our minds when we wade into these conversations, online or off. Melanie Green, an associate professor of communication at the University at Buffalo, has studied this question and found that people have a particularly hard time talking about issues on which there is no general consensus. Unknowns cause us anxiety, and when we perceive them to be connected to our identity in some way, even talking about them can feel like being threatened. This can be especially true between strangers, who don't know from the start what the other person's position—or disposition—might be.

Green and her colleagues did an experiment in which they presented participants with issues that people generally tend to agree on—food safety, support for veterans—as well as some that are more polarizing, like stem-cell research. The subjects were then asked to rate how threatening a computer-generated face with a neutral expression looked. They thought the face was a lot more threatening if they had just been presented with a polarizing issue.

Psychologist Linda Skitka and her colleagues at the University of Illinois at Chicago have come to an additional conclusion about why we have such trouble with conversations about politics and identity: a lot of us see these things as moral values, and those are starkly delineated in our minds. If we think something is either good or bad, moral or immoral, we're less likely to want to talk to someone who we believe falls on the "bad" or "immoral" side; the issue at hand is not a matter of opinion to us in that case, and we assume the interaction will be unpleasant or unnecessary.

After Grenny and Maxfield learned about respondents' broken relationships and fear of discussing politics, they asked about which elements went well in conversations with political adversaries. In response to that question, people used these words: *agree, listen, common, open, respect, think*, and *ask*. Think about the last time you talked to someone over social media, or in a comment thread on a website. Did it seem like there was a lot of agreeing or respecting going on? And (this one is a lot harder for me to answer) was anyone asking a genuine question?

Kids aren't immune to this dynamic either. They learn social skills and habits largely by watching their parents and other adults; if those adults are constantly absorbed in screens and getting upset or angry about what they're reading on those screens, it has an effect on the little ones. Brisa Ayub, a former senior producer of education content at Common Sense Media, told me the company has had to revise some of its guidelines to account for a whole new range of issues in recent years. Kids have learned all kinds of concerning new communication behaviors from watching adults and each other: bullying especially has taken on a whole new tone. Ayub hears a lot from parents and teachers of kids who suffer from FOMO—fear of missing out—when their so-called friends seem to purposely not invite them out but then tag them in photos of fun events that happened without them. Even the coveted "like" can be transformed into a bullying tool; aggressive liking—clicking "like" on *everything* a person posts or has ever posted—is a way of saying, "I'm watching you." Ayub pointed out that in this increasingly hostile digital environment, individual differences seem to have more power. "Those differences can be tapped into in so many different ways than they once were prior to these technologies," she said. "We no longer have to be face to face to showcase a power imbalance between two people."

Like me, she worries about what will come next. As app developers create new platforms, will they incorporate these concerns into the systems themselves? And in the meantime, will we learn to talk to each other with empathy?

We Need to Talk

The internet did not cause people to become rigid about rules of conversation, or even to gamify it. And neither did our most recent presidential election, however it may sometimes seem. Debate is an ancient form of conversation, and US political culture has long affected the way we talk to one another about controversial subjects. But the tension seemed heightened in the lead-up to the 2016 election, and at the end of the year, when it was finally over, our inability to empathize with each other only seemed to be getting worse. This left me feeling pretty hopeless about the future of online communication. It seemed like there were no good examples of how to do it right.

Journalist and conversational expert Celeste Headlee has some ideas. In 2017 she published a whole book about fixing conversations, called *We Need to Talk: How to Have Conversations That Matter*. When I called her to discuss it, she wanted to make one thing clear up front: "We are about to get a whole bunch of books and think pieces that blame tech for a lot of stuff going wrong and how we could have been so wrong about social media, and I feel like some of my work is going to be used to make that argument," she said. "I want to be clear first that tech is not the problem. It's a tool like any other tool."

We have just become so overwhelmed by the number of people and feelings and conversations this tool opens us up to that we've squandered our emotional energy, argues Headlee. She encourages people to establish common ground and try to combat the "horizontal" nature of many online relationships by having more one-on-one conversations. "Some of the best hope we have is that you aren't born with a specific amount of empathy," she reminded me. "We used to think you were either empathetic or you weren't, but the truth is you can increase your empathy, and one of the best and most effective ways is by hearing other people's perspectives and experiences."

I knew Headlee was right about the best way to increase empathy, and I could really feel the truth of what she said about emotional energy; by this point, I was exhausted. I ultimately had to step away from social media and turn to a different—and in some ways older—technology to find some hope.

At the time, I was walking to and from work, thirty minutes each way, and I'd been filling the time with podcasts. My typical interests tended toward the nerdy: science, politics, law. But during the 2016 campaign and in the wake of the election, I needed a break from the serious. I started listening to more conversational podcasts, like *Another Round* (hosted by Tracy Clayton and Heben Nigatu, two hilarious and clever black women writers working at BuzzFeed at the time), *Dear Sugars* (an advice podcast hosted by writers Cheryl Strayed and Steve Almond), and the ridiculous *My Dad Wrote a Porno* (a British podcast whose name is self-explanatory). Then in the summer of 2017 I came across *Conversations with People Who Hate Me*, hosted by writer and YouTuber Dylan Marron. I was still feeling a little raw, but I couldn't resist the title, so I dove in.

The first episode started with Marron stating the obvious to his guest:

"There's a lot that you and I disagree on."

"I know this," the guest said.

"As you know," Marron continued lightheartedly, "I'm a piece of shit."

"Let me take that back," the guest said, sounding both apologetic and amused at himself. "I didn't mean to call you a piece of shit . . . I apologize for calling you a piece of shit."

When I met Marron for coffee in Brooklyn about a year later, he raised his eyebrows when we talked about this point in the episode. He raises his eyebrows a lot—he's got an open, expressive face, and his hazel eyes are always searching to make contact. This particular eyebrow-raise seemed meant to convey *Isn't life wild?* Because what happened next on the podcast—what happens with most of Marron's guests—was that guest and host turned that insult into a pretty deep conversation that ended with them wishing each other well.

Marron started his career as more of a traditional artist and playwright, but he felt constrained by the theater world, where people often liked his ideas but didn't think they would work in that setting. So, like many millennials, he took to YouTube. He gained some fame from several viral YouTube series, including *Unboxing*, a satirical take on the trend in which people unpack deliveries of makeup, clothes, or toys on camera. In Marron's version, he "unboxed" concepts like police brutality and toxic masculinity (a popular term for the stereotypical norms associated with masculinity that limit men's emotional expression and, some theorists believe, contribute to violence against women). These videos, unsurprisingly, rubbed some people the wrong way.

Before the *Unboxing* videos, Marron had gone viral for *Every Single Word*, a video series in which he cut movies down to only the words spoken onscreen by people of color. He saw this as a way to highlight how Hollywood was "unfairly building empathy for only one type of person"—white people, mostly white men. When state laws prohibiting transgender people from using public restrooms that didn't match the sex on their birth certificates started to make headlines, Marron took his digital celebrity into those bathrooms, creating another series called

Sitting in Bathrooms with Trans People in which he did just that—sat in bathrooms with trans people and had conversations about all sorts of things, from gender identity and activism to celebrity culture and food. He sought to help people overcome the fear of what they didn't understand by demystifying the unknown.

These videos garnered Marron a lot of fans, but they also made some people really angry. I've written a lot about concerns over incivility on Facebook, Twitter, and Instagram, but the YouTube comment section can be a special kind of hell for content creators. There's an extra layer of vulnerability when people are responding not just to your words and ideas but to your face, your voice, and often your body all at once (even if the video has nothing to do with how you look). Marron admits he is not a saint in this regard—he has clapped back at his share of trolls, trying to turn the humiliation they seek back on them. But this got exhausting, and he ultimately realized he might be able to leverage some of this attention more productively. He started asking his meanest trolls if they'd be interested in talking in an old-fashioned way—on the phone—and having those conversations recorded for a podcast. To his surprise, some of them agreed.

In the first episode, Marron had a conversation with a man named Chris who had left the following comment on an *Unboxing* video about police brutality:

> When the police aren't there, sensitive young men like you will be the first to go. It's the people you are championing that hate you. One last message: you are talking with Muslim women, and told them to talk about the Muslim registry and how there was one with George Bush. You said a total lie that could have made them scared and made you look like a SJW and American men as monsters. You are

a piece of shit. Good thing no one watches you.
You say things that 100% make situations worse.

Marron called Chris via Skype and recorded their conversation. He told me he has unrecorded conversations with each of his guests first to make sure they're on the same page, that they understand it isn't a debate, and that he might have to edit out some "ums" and "uhs." When I asked, over coffee, whether he felt it was necessary to explain the editing process to people who probably don't like the media, Marron pushed back a little.

"All of my guests feel so varied," he said. "I don't think any of them are alike to each other." Translation: I was making unfair assumptions about the people who made unfair assumptions about him. He reminded me how unnatural empathy can feel, especially when the topic is politics and identity. But Marron has had so many of these conversations now, it seems as if empathy comes more naturally to him than judgment.

Maybe that's why the conversation in the first episode of his podcast started with him asking Chris how his day had been. Chris said he'd been fixing his car and washing machine. You could hear him shoo his dogs out of the room.

As they got into the meat of the conversation, Chris explained that when he made his "piece of shit" comment, he had been drinking. He stood by most of what he said but clarified that he meant it more generally about "SJWs" ("social-justice warriors," or people who advocate for social-justice issues on the internet). SJWs, Chris explained, "want to turn over the whole country in order to solve small problems." His primary example: the LGBTQ community. He's a supporter of gay marriage, but the way he sees it, gay people have "always been getting along fine in life [and] they don't need a whole list of rights. They're people. That's like saying redheaded rights. It seems silly to me."

Marron, who identifies as queer, simply listened politely. He had
called this man to understand his point of view. As it turned out, Chris's
wife was a big fan of Marron and his videos. What had really set Chris
off was when Marron said it was racist to cite crime statistics in the black
community as a partial explanation for police brutality. The two men
discussed the issue back and forth for a few minutes. Chris sounded
like he didn't think racism was much of an issue in twenty-first-century
America but admitted he could be wrong. Marron asked how it felt
to be called racist. When the conversation turned to immigration, he
attempted to build a bridge with Chris over their shared immigrant
heritage.

When Chris had watched Marron's videos, he'd seen him as a
twenty-two-year-old know-it-all, a representative of the SJW crowd,
who he assumed were mostly "rich college student[s] who [have their]
mom and daddy pay for everything, and they pick and choose these
subjects to be angry about in a world where people really generally don't
have that much to be angry about." But after talking to Marron (who
was twenty-eight at the time), Chris said he thought that Marron as an
individual was a "fine young man . . . just misguided."

I found myself pretty engrossed in this conversation, and I realized
it wasn't just because I cared deeply about the subject matter. It was
because I had never heard this kind of disagreement play out in such a
civil way, especially after beginning with such hostility. I tried to imagine seeing the same conversation in the comments on a Facebook post.
I realized that in pixels, Chris would probably seem like just another
troll to me. On the phone, he was a man named Chris with a wife and
two kids who had worked as a CT-scan technologist for forty-five years,
and who had been a liberal until, at thirty-five, he read some books
that convinced him life begins at conception. In other words, he was a
complex person, just like Marron, and just like me.

"It can feel weird to be empathizing with someone you profoundly
disagree with," Marron said when we met, "especially in an age when

people say you're just as bad as them if you empathize with them. But all my guests . . . I think they're just good people trying to do the best they can. We all have these really different experiences, different things that drive us to be who we are. That's largely what divides us, and how we present that version of ourselves online is where all this comes from."

I didn't sympathize with Chris. He didn't convince me of anything. I didn't acquire his worldview, but this was one of the first times I'd been able to understand one like it. And it seemed like a similar thing was happening between him and Marron. Chris had criticized the Black Lives Matter movement and activism in the LGBTQ community, and Marron pushed back, but there was something—maybe the tone of Marron's voice, or the fact that these two people had agreed at the beginning that this would be a civil conversation—that allowed it to get real without going off the rails. Chris seemed to be examining Marron's perspective as much as Marron was examining Chris's, and by the end, even though it was clear they were still very far apart ideologically, instead of calling Marron a piece of shit, Chris called him "pal."

At the end of each episode, Marron asks his guests whether the conversation changed them in any way. "I no longer hate you," Chris said, laughing. "You won."

"It's not about winning or losing!" Marron protested.

"You're willing to listen. That's the important thing," Chris said. "I tell you what, I'm going to listen, because it's important." And he gave Marron a final order: "Keep up the bad work."

The Magic of Listening

Not all the guests on *Conversations with People Who Hate Me* are as civil as Chris, but they all have a few things in common (in addition to having trolled Dylan Marron): they agreed to talk to him one-on-one, to learn something about him, and to be a little bit vulnerable themselves. They agreed to a set of rules—the main one being "This is not a debate"—and mostly followed them. And by turning hateful online comments into real offline conversations, then broadcasting those conversations via a different digital medium (podcasting), Marron and his guests aren't just talking about empathy—they're modeling it for a captive audience that can't respond in a knee-jerk way.

Conversations with People Who Hate Me isn't the only podcast trying to bridge the divide between people who hold differing views. I was nearly stopped in my tracks while walking home from work one day in 2017 as I listened to longtime Republican strategist Rick Wilson talk to progressive commentator and writer Ana Marie Cox on her podcast *With Friends Like These*. I was surprised to hear Cox, a staunch anti-Trumper, chatting with this big-R Republican about the current state of social issues, which they clearly didn't agree on. But they were being so *civil*. I couldn't have a conversation like that with anyone in my life. Even the people close to me who differed politically either were uninterested in discussing politics and social issues, or tended to make such conversations into, well, debates or games (even offline). But here was an example of how to do it—how to *actually* "agree to disagree" without destroying a relationship or giving too much ground on your most closely held beliefs. Maybe I should have been embarrassed for feeling so amazed by this at the ripe age of twenty-eight, but remember, I'm a child of the internet. Sometimes it feels like we need to see (well, hear) examples of this happening or we might forget it's even possible.

Listening to conversations like this can help create empathy in a couple of ways. For one thing, they're people telling stories, and multiple studies have shown that people who read more stories (especially literary fiction) score higher on empathy tests. But it turns out there's some more science to why listening alone—as opposed to reading or watching a story or even being right next to someone as they speak— can have a particular effect on empathy.

A recent study seemed to prove what those of us familiar with online debates have feared for years: people we disagree with seem less human to us when we read their views than when we hear them spoken aloud. In an experiment conducted by researchers at the University of California, Berkeley, people who only listened to others describe their views on issues like abortion and the US war in Afghanistan rated the speakers as more "humanlike" than those they could see as well as hear, and those whose opinions they simply read. The researchers found similar results when they exposed subjects to other people's views on 2016 US presidential candidates: subjects saw people they disagreed with as more sophisticated and warmer than those they agreed with, when they could only hear their voices.

"Whereas existing research demonstrates that cues in speech increase accurate understanding of mental states, our experiments demonstrate that a person's voice reveals something more fundamental: the presence of a humanlike mind capable of thinking and feeling," the authors wrote.

In 2017, Michael W. Kraus of Yale University and some fellow researchers conducted another study in which three hundred subjects were exposed to three different scenarios involving two women teasing each other back and forth. Some could only see the interaction, some could only hear it, and some could both see and hear. The researchers then asked the subjects to guess how each of the women felt, rating them on emotions like happiness, embarrassment, disgust, empathy, enthusiasm, fear, and guilt, on a scale from "Not at all" to "A great deal." (Teasing, it turns out, "activates a broad range of positive and negative emotions, making it a particularly relevant domain for testing empathic accuracy.") The researchers scored the subjects based on the difference between their estimates of the women's emotions and the women's self-reported feelings; a lower score meant better empathic accuracy. Those who could only hear the teasing got the lowest (best) scores, suggesting that there was something about voice—the way it's expressed or the way we process it—that triggers empathy in a way that seeing facial expressions (a more typical measure of empathic accuracy) doesn't. In other experiments, the researchers found that people who had a conversation in a dark room were better at guessing each other's mental state, and people who listened to others talk in a dark room were better at it than those who could see the people they were listening to.

The researchers had predicted this might happen, for a few reasons. One: voices convey emotion, both through the content of what a person says and in the way they say it. "Both sources of information contained in the voice provide access to the internal emotional states of others," they wrote. And two: Kraus made another important observation, that intimacy can change everything in these contexts. Seeing someone's face all the time creates a kind of expertise that allows a person to understand another's mental state just by looking at them. This could also mean that the benefit of voice-only communication when it comes to empathic accuracy is only enjoyed by strangers, but there seems to be a middle ground between complete stranger and best friend or family member where empathic conversations happen most naturally. This finding could help explain why listening to Dylan Marron talk to semi-strangers who yelled at him on the internet felt so instructive and even cathartic to me.

Marron's work seems to be having an impact. He told me he gets a lot of emails from people who say listening to his conversations has helped them in their own online and IRL interactions, especially with their parents. He gets tagged in Twitter conversations by listeners who were inspired by him to call people who've sent them nasty emails. Mostly, people write to tell him that after listening, they feel a little better about the world.

Still, he isn't sanguine about the future of human interaction via the internet. He's gotten plenty of hate from people he agrees with as well as those on the "other side"—he even named one *Conversations with People Who Hate Me* episode "The Call Is Coming from Inside the

House." He's afraid people will continue to move further and further into their own "ideological pods." But he also has a lot of hope. He sees a future in which we are able to harness the ways the social web helps mobilize people and get crucial information out quickly, while we also get better at diagnosing and treating problems like trolling and lack of verification.

"I want us to move toward a system where we are operating on at least a shared pool of truth rather than separate truths we can all link to," he told me. "I hope we will continue to pinpoint the best of the internet while also creating more and more spaces for us to move conversations offline, more spaces for us to speak one-on-one without being upvoted or downvoted."

He also told me the show has made him rethink his own approach to social media. When I asked him about this, he pondered for a second, then said, "I think I'm never going to screenshot a negative comment about me and make fun of their typos again." He said he doesn't find it productive to get into heated online arguments anymore in general. He prefers to take things offline, even when he's not recording. I pointed out the irony of this for someone who built his career on the internet, but as a millennial who grew up online, I get it. I too have sought ways to take conversations about tough issues offline to work things out, so that when the same thing happens again, I'm more ready to approach them with empathy.

I still wondered if it was possible to have this transformation *on* social media, where we are increasingly conducting our lives.

Engineering Better Conversations

In 2014, I wrote for the *Columbia Journalism Review* about a research project that aimed to make comment sections less hostile. The website of the Raleigh, North Carolina, newspaper the *News & Observer* served as a testing ground for a new tool being developed at Michigan State University that would analyze the language used in online conversations and pinpoint when they went off the rails. The folks at the *News & Observer* and other newspapers wanted to understand how they could better moderate conversations in the comment sections of their articles and encourage healthier debate; the Michigan State researchers wanted to see what their algorithm could do. So they put it to the test, gathering raw data from two hours of commenting on one *N&O* op-ed about tax issues facing same-sex couples. They coded words and phrases for their usefulness (facilitating good conversation) or detriment (shutting others down or baiting trolls). The results of the analysis showed that phrases like "Let me see if I'm understanding this correctly" and "To clear up a few misconceptions" had the most positive impact.

The creators of tools like this—and there are increasingly more of them—say they don't want them to be used to censor people; they want moderators or onlookers to be able to "rescue" conversations before they derail, and participants to self-correct when necessary. This approach can seem kind of clunky and mechanical, and the explicit goal isn't empathy building, it's keeping people engaged and coming back to spend more time (and click on more things) on a website. I had been skeptical about how useful this technology would be, and even more uncertain that it would tell me anything about empathy.

Then, a few years later, I came across the Michigan State project again. It had become Faciloscope, an app built by the university in partnership with the Science Museum of Minnesota and North Carolina's Museum of Life and Science. It uses a natural-language-processing algorithm that analyzes sentences and interprets them based on three basic conversational "rhetorical moves": staging (laying out the ground rules for a conversation), evoking (pointing out relationships between participants, e.g., "as Kaitlin said to Reid . . ."), and inviting (directly soliciting participation by asking a question or requesting a comment). The idea is that by identifying where these things are happening in the conversation, in real time, a moderator might be able to see where the interaction could go wrong.

Importantly, Faciloscope and other bots like it aren't evaluating the *content* of what people are saying, just the *structure* of the conversation. There are obvious limitations with this approach; for instance, most people don't enter comment threads expecting a structured debate or thinking too hard about "rhetorical moves." The app is made for moderators and facilitators of online comment sections, but the creators have said it could also be useful for social media, so I decided to try it out.

When I discovered Faciloscope, I happened to have just participated in a tense conversation in the comments of a post in a Facebook group about books (like I said, debates pop up everywhere and can be hard to ignore!). The original poster had told a story about removing offensive books from free library boxes in her neighborhood and recycling them, sparking a debate about censorship. It got heated pretty quickly, but at first glance it wasn't easy to tell why. I copied the text of a chunk of the conversation and pasted it into the Faciloscope text box after deleting the metadata (like the time, the date, people's names—except first names when they were used to "evoke") and also emojis and hashtags, so as not to confuse the algorithm.

Ironically, before I could proceed, I had to click a box assuring the program that I was "not a robot" and play a little matching game to prove it. Once that was out of the way, I clicked "Analyze" and waited a few seconds. A pie chart popped up, showing me the stats: 69.23 percent of the pie was chartreuse, the color that signified "staging"; 23.08 percent was "inviting" (purple); and 7.69 percent was "evoking" (blue). I was also able to see a "move pattern," showing the order that each "move" came in. There was a lot of chartreuse concentrated in four major areas, with three little purple bars and only one blue.

Like I said, I'd been skeptical. But when I saw all that greenish-yellow, I felt a little green myself because of what it seemed to suggest: that the three of us in this conversation had apparently spent most of our time setting up, and re-setting up, our own positions and expectations. That didn't leave much time for showing that we understood—or even acknowledged the existence of—each other's points of view. I was looking at this analysis after the fact, but I could easily see how doing this in the middle of a discussion might make me think twice about what to say next.

Google has a similar tool called Perspective API. On the website showing off how it works, there are two main examples. One has sorted comments about climate change, Brexit, and the most recent US presidential election and rated them based on perceived toxicity, a measurement derived from responses to a survey in which people were asked to identify words and phrases that they deemed "rude, disrespectful, or unreasonable" and that would likely make them leave a discussion. In the other example, Google used the same survey to power a "Writing Experiment" bot using Perspective API. I plugged in a few phrases and it spit back percentages, estimating how toxic they were likely to be perceived in an online conversation:

The message from my former classmate, YOU HAVE NO RIGHT TO JUDGE US OR OUR ACTIONS, came back at 0.12, "Unlikely to be perceived toxic." (The algorithm apparently didn't take all caps into account.)

And You are a piece of shit, from Dylan Marron's commenter, Chris, came back at .99, "Likely to be perceived as toxic," while You say things that 100% make situations worse was deemed only 35 percent likely to be perceived as toxic.

A few months later I tried the same phrases again; the all-caps comment and the "piece of shit" comment came back at the same level of toxicity as before, but the last one was now much less likely to be perceived as toxic, according to Perspective API. This might be because, as a machine-learning algorithm, it learns and changes based on the input it receives.

These results are informed by survey answers from one group of people, and they obviously don't take context into account. But there is some evidence that tools like this may actually be able to help predict—and eventually prevent—toxic conversations.

Researchers at Cornell University conducted a study using a mixture of Google's Perspective API and human intelligence to test predictions of when conversations might go sour. They analyzed 1,270 conversations in Wikipedia editors' forums that had begun civilly enough but devolved into hostility (they used Perspective API to measure "toxicity"). They lined up these conversations with ones on the same topic that went well and found that when the first comment in an exchange used direct questions or started sentences with "you," the conversation was significantly more likely to go awry. Comments that started with gratitude, greetings, or attempts at coordination were correlated with conversations staying on track. It wasn't that only people who agreed were nice to one another; disagreeing seemed to be OK as long as it was done using "hedges" and prompts for opinion. The research also supported the long-held idea that using "I/we" sentences tends to keep people from getting too defensive.

This study was unique in that it measured conversations between collaborators—people who were working together to edit Wikipedia pages—and not total strangers. But the most interesting takeaway may be the success rates of humans vs. bots. In this study, Perspective API correctly predicted how a conversation would turn out 60.5 percent of the time. The humans were right 72 percent of the time. The combination of Perspective API and the researchers' additional analysis was right 64.9 percent of the time.

"We, as humans, have an intuition of whether a conversation is about to go awry, but it's often just a suspicion," Cristian Danescu-Niculescu-Mizil, assistant professor of information sciences and coauthor of the paper, said at the time. "We can't do it 100 percent of the time. We wonder if we can build systems to replicate or even go beyond this intuition."

The data gathered by these algorithms has the potential to help us remember to take a breath before we enter or continue a conversation, and to act as a reminder that we already have the tools to guess when more empathy might be needed. Sometimes we just need a little nudge.

But as we've seen, there's a growing concern among experts that young people aren't building empathy—or learning how to harness it—at the levels they should be. This shortfall is troubling enough in regular conversation, but as the tech we use to facilitate our communications gets stronger, the empathy we have in reserve to draw on will need to be stronger too. How do we make sure kids are prepared for the conversations of the future? I went in search of the people whose job it is to figure that out.

CHAPTER 2
TEACHING THEM YOUNG

The video opens on a young girl with shiny hair and a big smile sitting at a table with a box in front of her. The setup is similar to that of any unboxing video, in which YouTubers open packages and discuss the contents for the entertainment of their subscribers. This video is different, though; the item in the package doesn't really exist—at least, not yet.

I watch as the girl removes two items: a pink wristband that looks kind of like a Fitbit activity tracker, and a matching headset that reminds me of the headphones I used to wear to listen to my portable CD player. The FeelThat system, the girl explains, will detect changes in her hormones and analyze her voice for emotion. When she's ready, she can switch a privacy setting on the device to "Public" and it will transmit her feelings—her actual feelings, not just information about them—to her connections on a network of other FeelThat users.

She seems a little nervous as she gets set up to try the system, but the overall tone of the video is excitement. The Institute for the Future (IFTF), a Palo Alto think tank, created the scenario as part of an online multiplayer game called Face the Future, developed to teach middle- and high-school students to think critically about the impact of technology on their lives—now and in the future. The game, which launched just after the 2016 presidential election, asked players to imagine a future in which a device like the FeelThat is as commonplace as a smartphone. "Who would you share your FeelThat data with?" the game asked. "Whose data would you want to see?"

When Calee Prindle, then a ninth-grade English teacher at the Facing History School in the Hell's Kitchen neighborhood of New York City, queued up the FeelThat video to show her class, many of her students were feeling vulnerable. The presidential campaign and election had been emotionally stressful for the diverse student body; many felt personally threatened by the rhetoric and policy proposals of newly elected President Trump. Prindle told me that she had been planning to spend two days preparing her students for the Face the Future game, explaining the concept of empathy and how it relates to the way we use technology. But after the election, she scrapped her plans and instead spent an entire day addressing the elephant in the room. Then, the political drama and its potential impacts on their own lives still top-of-mind, the students dove into the game.

Using their own feelings as a guide, her students considered the big questions that parents, teachers, and pundits had been discussing for months: Can we ever truly understand the way another person feels? Should we bother trying? And then they went beyond: What if a Trump supporter—or Trump himself—could literally feel what a Mexican immigrant was feeling as they approached the border? What if we could all feel what it was like to stand at a lectern in the White House and address the nation? What if a police officer could feel the fear of a black man during a traffic stop? What if that man could feel what was coursing through the cop's veins too? What if it was all out in the open, in the cloud—not words about feelings, but the feelings themselves? What might be fixed? What could go wrong?

The students in Prindle's class, plus thousands of others who logged in to the game from around the world, started by watching a series of videos that ranged from endearing (the young girl excitedly unwrapping her FeelThat) to disturbing (a young man receiving his girlfriend's feelings in real time as she dies in a car accident). Then the players answered questions—some with an optimistic theme (labeled "Positive Imagination") and some for those who were more skeptical or concerned about the concept (labeled "Shadow Imagination"). "What would *you* want to do in this future?" for example, and "What could go wrong with the FeelThat Network?" Players' answers showed up in a feed where others could express their encouragement with an "upvote" (similar to a Facebook or Twitter "like" or "favorite") or comment. Players earned "foresight points" for engagement with others, while a moderator ensured that bullying and trolling didn't derail the game. The interface highlighted the comments with the most engagement in real time, so players (and other observers like myself) could see which hypotheses were getting the most attention.

Participants' comments built on each other to create a visual representation of the conversation as it unfolded. Many were worried or fearful:

> "This could start a war!"

> "It could create more separation. We have racism based on physical traits. What if we discriminated based on emotional traits?"

> "I worry about privacy. I am currently concerned about phones tracking our locations. What will future governments do with FeelThat data?"

But some saw an empathic opportunity:

"People could become friends based on having the same emotions about the same things."

"What an opportunity to show people with empathy deficiency how certain things literally feel."

After two days of play, there was a deep web of concern and excitement about the future of technology—and of empathy.

In class, some of Prindle's students started thinking out loud about how important it was to pause before typing or speaking. Others questioned the goals of the game's creators. After the game, one student approached Prindle confused, saying she'd thought they had been done talking about the election in class. She'd begun to associate discussions about thinking before you speak and putting yourself in others' shoes with discussions about American politics.

"They made that connection with talking about the importance of trying to understand people's perspective[s] and hear people out," Prindle told me later. "That's empathy."

The game was fun. I played a bit myself, choosing different "Positive Imagination" and "Shadow Imagination" scenarios, and imagining a world in which, instead of explaining myself with my most comfortable mode of expression—words—I could (or maybe even had to) simply press a button and transmit how I felt. But I knew something many of the students didn't yet know: it was more than just a thought experiment. Technology makes it easier every day to communicate without much effort, and there are already products in the works whose stated purpose is similar to that of the FeelThat. The fact is, teenagers like those in Prindle's classroom could be the ones using this technology for real within the next few decades—if they aren't the ones making it. Considering the many concerned responses and worst-case scenarios in the game, it could be a scary proposition. We aren't ready. But if we take a step back, these concerns about hypothetical technology are not much different from what parents and educators are worrying about in the present: what the technology we already have might be doing to their kids' ability to empathize.

Studies show that teaching traits like kindness, compassion, and empathy, in an explicit and intentional way at a young age, can make a difference. A 2011 meta-analysis of social-emotional learning, which many US curricula have embraced in recent decades, suggested that it led to higher graduation rates and safer sex, even eighteen years later. Clinical psychologist Lisa Flook and teacher Laura Pinger have studied the effects of a "kindness curriculum" on preschool-aged kids and found that twelve weeks of mindfulness and lessons about social-emotional development led to marked improvements compared to a control group, whose members were more selfish over time.

The idea of teaching empathy in schools is not new, though openness and creativity about it have grown in recent times. For decades, a Canadian organization called Roots of Empathy has been bringing babies into classrooms with the intent of illustrating this skill. The program enlists neighborhood parents to bring their babies to a classroom once every three weeks, allowing students to observe and try to label the baby's feelings. This activity, according to Roots of Empathy, helps kids learn to recognize emotions and understand that they aren't the only ones who feel things—an important social-emotional milestone. By 2001, according to a study commissioned by the government of Manitoba, students who observed Roots of Empathy babies showed improvement in social behavior, physical aggression, and indirect aggression, both immediately and in the years after participating. The program has also been used in the US, where several studies have found similar effects.

Apps, games, and virtual-reality experiences are the latest evolution of empathy education. Classrooms around the country now have tablets stocked with interactive lessons on kindness, integrity, empathy, and understanding. But with new educational tools come new responsibilities and concerns. Even as they turn to tech to help teach soft skills, parents and teachers worry about how much time children are spending in front of screens.

John Medina, director of Seattle Pacific University's Brain Center for Applied Research, writes in his book *Attack of the Teenage Brain! Understanding and Supporting the Weird and Wonderful Adolescent Learner* about how difficult it is to find straight answers about tech's impact on kids. He shares two pieces of research on the impact of video games on kids. One found that playing video games caused problems paying attention later on; the other said video games were great tools for research facilities because they *helped* kids pay attention. Even social media, as Medina found (and as we'll continue to see throughout this book), has a dual nature when it comes to brains of all ages.

In one 2016 study, ten-to-fourteen-year-olds who used Twitter and Facebook saw improvement on the Adolescent Measure of Empathy and Sympathy, a test used by psychologists to measure kids' cognitive and affective empathy and sympathy levels. The researchers found that the teenagers improved in both cognitive empathy (understanding others' feelings) and affective empathy (sharing those feelings, putting themselves in others' shoes). On the other hand, recent research has also shown increased levels of narcissism among people who post on Facebook a lot, and narcissism doesn't go well with empathy. Though it's clear that teaching empathy and kindness to kids can pay off, Medina and most other researchers in this field aren't ready to say for sure whether technology is to blame for kids' lack of empathy, or whether it can be used to help fix the problem, or both.

"Controlling the variables necessary to obtain a clear view will take *years*," Medina writes.

But plenty of teachers and parents feel like something more needs to be done in the meantime, and they can tell that some things seem to help their kids, regardless of the data. Developers like Raul Gutierrez aren't wasting any time.

Brain Games

Gutierrez, who cofounded a company called Tinybop that makes educational tech for kids, worries about young people missing something big while they're immersed in digital games, but still thinks those games may be one of the best ways to reach them. When we spoke on the phone, he started with an observation that he thought illustrated how subtle this problem can be.

One of the first things a group of kids will do when they enter Minecraft, the popular building-and-exploration computer game, is to play hide-and-seek, he said. "Kids come home after school, they all log on, and they play the same thing they used to play in person, but digitally."

In a way, this is a relief, because it means kids are still interacting the way they always have, despite concerns about technology causing isolation. But there's a key difference: in a real game of hide-and-seek, players can have the formative experience of going too far. Everyone of a certain age has accidentally hurt someone's feelings or hit or kicked another kid during a game like this, and when that happened, they could see it on the other person's face. They were in such close proximity, they couldn't avoid having a reaction. While a sense of community might exist in a digital space, that kind of accountability often doesn't. Most video games for kids focus on solving puzzles or winning points, which is fine, but as Gutierrez said, it doesn't really compare to what happens when you're playing a family game of Monopoly and your little sister upends the board when she realizes she's losing.

When Gutierrez's son was in fourth grade, Instagram swept through the class. Gutierrez told his son that he needed to use his real name on social media and understand that, just like him, everyone he talked to there was a real person with real feelings and should be treated kindly.

"What I found was that when he got on there, he was still an eight-year-old, posting about origami and a really delicious bagel he ate," Gutierrez said.

Meanwhile, his thirteen-year-old has entered the fraught world of YouTube, where he has his own channel that he uses to share Minecraft videos. He's made some real friends there, said Gutierrez, including one young girl who reached out to him for help when someone else harassed her on the site. The boy and his friends reported the harasser without any parental intervention.

"The kids are all right," Gutierrez said. We just have to give them a little guidance.

Research shows that kids are growing up with less ability to concentrate, more anxiety, and less self-esteem thanks to social media, and they don't have as many opportunities to learn social-emotional skills in real life.

Still, many parents embrace allowing kids to use technology at younger and younger ages. One study found that 90 percent of two-year-olds knew how to use tablets, and if you eat out at restaurants you've probably seen kids even younger than that being pacified by cartoons on tiny screens as their parents try to eat in peace.

This might not necessarily be a bad thing, but there's a growing urgency to make sure we are at least doing it with intention. If kids are going to have their faces glued to screens regardless, many parents, teachers, and technologists have begun trying to use that same technology to meet their kids where they are with lessons in kindness, empathy, and compassion, so that when they have difficult real-life experiences—and they will, at least for now—they're prepared.

In fact, there are plenty of anecdotes about kids bucking the stereotypes and taking real steps toward improving empathy and compassion among themselves and their peers. In 2018 I read about an eighth-grader in Renton, Washington, named Welela Solomon, who was making the tech-conference circuit talking about artificial intelligence and empathy. Thanks in part to a Microsoft-sponsored school curriculum focused on the marriage of tech and social skills, Solomon and her classmates developed a presentation on the relevance of history to our current struggles with creating an empathetic culture around technology. "AI is not all bad," she told the *Renton Reporter* in February 2018. "It can be bad, but it can also be good. It has changed over time. If we use it to make our world a better place it's going to help a lot."

One hot June afternoon in 2018, I took a spin on the Tinybop app Homes, which allows kids to explore illustrated versions of different kinds of living spaces, from a typical American house to a Mongolian *ger*. I decided to start with a visit to an animated Guatemalan home. The first things I heard when I arrived were animal sounds—chickens, pigs, goats. I also noticed how colorful all the buildings were. Once inside the small house, I instinctively looked for things that were familiar to me. I found a radio and sewing machine similar to the ones my grandparents had in their (American) house, some flip-flops like the ones in my own closet, and a few pieces of furniture. Inside a crib was a little doll, and hanging on one wall was a power strip. Only small things marked the cultural differences between this home and my own: a book about anatomy that I picked up and leafed through was all in Spanish; a working loom sat in one corner; and in the kitchen, instead of a stove there was a hot plate. Books and toys and personal effects were scattered about. Using the simple controls, I tidied up, putting some pillows into a box on the floor. Outside, I helped plant some beans and washed dishes in a big yellow basin. I was even able to fill up the basin with water until the bowls and soap floated to the top.

The app wouldn't strike most adults—or even many kids—as extraordinary. Anyone who has played any kind of mobile or video game knows to expect that some things can be picked up and moved, some will make noise, and some will sit frustratingly inert no matter how many times you tap the screen. But an aspect that is ancillary to many games—the fact that the player is experiencing another "place"— is the whole point in this one.

My next stop was the American house. I had given the app permission to use my camera, and when I walked into a bedroom with a mirror, I saw myself reflected back. To an adult, the metaphor can seem a little too obvious, but imagine being a kid who has never been in an American house (or a Guatemalan or Yemeni one, for that matter) and seeing yourself in one, on the small screen in front of you. That's a level of perspective-taking not available from many other sources.

I wondered whether some kids might take this all too literally, assuming everyone in Guatemala or the US lived the same way. But Gutierrez explained to me that the goal is really just to trigger further curiosity. When I played, I started to wonder: Did the people who lived in houses like this grow all their own food? Did they have to, or was that a choice? What kind of food was in that pot on the hot plate? Why did they wash outside? There was an outhouse in the yard—maybe there was no indoor plumbing here?

Gutierrez told me about a letter his team at Tinybop got from the mother of a young Muslim girl from Yemen. The family had immigrated to the US several years before, and the girl had very little memory of the place where she was born. Unfortunately, the mother wrote, while she thought of Yemen as a beautiful place, depictions of the country— where much of their extended family still lived—were often negative, showing war and terrorism and poverty, and her daughter didn't want to share this part of her story with friends. Then the girl's class started using Homes. After looking through a Yemeni tower house in the app, the girl was suddenly proud to bring her iPad to school to show her friends what her grandmother's house looked like. It was the first time, the mother said, that her daughter had been proud of where she was from, and her friends were eager to see how it was both different from their own homes and the same.

Gutierrez said that when kids play Homes, they inevitably find the kitchen in every house and make food, find toys and play with them, and look for the bathroom so they can try to flush something down the toilet. They also learn lessons about expectations, identity, and self-awareness, concepts he's been trying to figure out how to teach since his own childhood experiences of being seen as "different" in East Texas, a place he described as "profoundly divided," in the 1970s and '80s.

"There was literally a train track running through the town, and on one side was the white section and on the other side the black section," he told me.

Gutierrez and his family didn't really fit in on either side of the tracks—his father was from Mexico and his mother was a New Yorker of Irish American descent. He himself was born in Mexico, but felt he looked more like his mother. This "outsider" role, he said, gave him a unique perspective on the racially charged atmosphere of his community. When kids from different backgrounds would fight and people would get hurt, he was always on the margins, observing and wondering why others acted the way they did. He didn't see the divisions that other people saw, and it made him interested in why people see the world in different ways.

Gutierrez's wife, who is from Korea, tells him he has bad *nunchi*—a Korean cultural concept of being able to listen to and identify the moods of those around you. The way Gutierrez put it, there's an expectation that one is "supremely aware of everything that's happening with everybody in the group." It's an extreme form of empathy, Gutierrez said, and it informs culture in an ineffable way. For example, someone at a dinner table in Korea would be unlikely to say, "Look at the time, I have to go!"—they'd wait until it was clear that everyone was ready. For a Westerner, even one who's been observing and trying to understand the people around him for most of his life, there's a learning curve.

With Tinybop, Gutierrez is trying to make the learning curve for empathy, in a world consumed by technology, a little smoother. At a certain age (experts say between nine months and around two years old) empathy starts kicking in for kids. At this point they start to respond with sadness when another child gets hurt, or with happiness when something good happens to someone else, rather than getting distracted or ignoring the other person. Gutierrez hopes Tinybop's apps will make that switch happen sooner and encourage kids to employ empathy more intentionally through the use of technology, without distracting them with bells and whistles. It's a delicate balance. "We're designing for slowness in an age of speed," he told me.

Sara Konrath, the University of Michigan researcher who released the 2010 headline-grabbing analysis about declining empathy among college students, has created her own empathy-teaching app for kids, called Random App of Kindness. Konrath, whose previous research suggested a connection between smartphones and empathy decline, has said she still believes phones can present an opportunity to teach social skills. Working with tech developers, her research team built an app with nine games that help kids learn how to recognize others' emotions, care for animals and babies in need, resolve conflicts, take others' perspectives, and cooperate.

One benefit of researchers creating an app is that they can figure out pretty quickly whether it's working. Konrath's team studied 106 kids between the ages of ten and seventeen and found that after two months of using Random App of Kindness, they were more likely to help others and less likely to resort to anger and aggression. On the blog for the game, she said her team is working on guides for parents and teachers, but she hopes that in the meantime pediatricians will recommend Random App of Kindness as a tool for building empathy and other social skills in a way kids are already comfortable with.

For some education-technology companies, empathy is baked into the process of creating. Ami Shah, CEO and cofounder of Canadian education-technology company Peekapak, started a business for the same reason a lot of entrepreneurs do—she wanted others to have a different experience than she'd had herself. At a young age, Shah became an activist on the issues of violence against women and among students, inspired in part by the Columbine High School shootings, which happened when she was a kid, and in part by her own and her peers' experiences. This activism sometimes involved giving talks to her high-school classmates. When we spoke on the phone, she told me about one formative incident that still stands out. As she started to give a talk about violence against women to one class, a male classmate piped up: "That's a stupid topic. The woman probably deserved it."

"I thought, that kind of ignorance cannot live in the community that I live in, that I go to school in," she said.

Shah spent some time in the corporate world, but she kept thinking about that moment and about some experiences her peers and family members had—her mother getting robbed at knifepoint, friends being harassed. She saw a lot of negativity in the world, but she was still convinced education could be a tool to drive change. After reading a moving story about the importance of instilling a sense of curiosity, wonder, and creativity in young children, Shah and cofounder Angie Chan started collaborating with educators on narrative-driven social-skills education. With some venture capital, that collaboration became Peekapak, a company that offers books and games similar to those offered by Tinybop, but with both animals and humans as main characters.

In one Peekapak game, the student creates an avatar to help Leo the hedgehog overcome various challenges. As they do that, they become friends with him and get invited to his house. Spending time in hedgehog world is cute and entertaining for kids, but Peekapak's research shows it actually helps them learn perspective-taking for other humans as well. Another core component of the game is self-awareness. It's hard for kids to identify and respond to others' emotions if they can't figure out their own.

There are dozens of similar apps, though few have the same research backing. Some schools that can afford the technology have also branched out into virtual reality, allowing kids to "visit" places like ancient Egypt or modern-day Syria to get at least a taste of what these places—and the lives of the people who live there—are like. There are many reasons for skepticism about VR: it is still relatively expensive, especially when trying to scale it for in-school use, and to many parents it just seems like playing games. In the spring of 2018, Common Sense Media and Stanford University released a report on parents' views of VR's impact on kids. Thirty-eight percent of those who responded to the research survey thought VR would help children empathize with people different from themselves. Among parents of eight-to-seventeen-year-olds, the percentage was fifty-six.

Michael Robb, senior director of research at Common Sense Media, wasn't surprised that parents were relatively skeptical about this, but he thinks the research is more promising. He pointed to several studies that show VR can help with perspective-taking, a precursor to empathy.

The Common Sense Media research came out of the Virtual Human Interaction Lab at Stanford, where Jeremy Bailenson has been working on VR and empathy for several years. In 2009, one of his studies found that elementary-aged kids were so immersed in a VR experience about orca whales that they later thought they had really swum with them. In 2017, Bailenson and researchers at the Sesame Network showed that kids treated VR Grover more like a real-life friend than when they saw him on TV or online.

At Girls Academic Leadership Academy (known as GALA), California's first all-girl STEM academy, in Los Angeles, high-school students in VR producer Robyn Janz's after-school program are learning to build their own virtual experiences about social issues like mental health and homelessness, which they then share with the United Way.

"These girls are twelve. Imagine what the world will look like ten years from now when they enter the workforce in their chosen field," Janz said. "One of them told me she wants to become a doctor, and she's now planning on using VR to create experiences that can help her treat people."

Something else Janz said in our interview has stuck with me. "Here's how I look at it: VR empathy is a fantastic experience built on irony. You go through something that is anywhere from completely joyous and euphoric to absolutely catastrophic and cataclysmic. How you come out of immersion is more to do with your subjective experience in life than anything else."

Educational apps and experiences can be cute and informative. They often seem not just benign, but beneficial. But they are still apps and games—they're played on smartphones and other devices that allow users' activity to be tracked. Developers argue that kind of surveillance is necessary to know whether the tools are working, and many companies do anonymize the data they collect. But as the market for education technology grows larger, and the tech itself grows more complex, feel-good tech tools can sometimes feel simultaneously sinister.

Ethical EdTech

One popular empathy-building app used by teachers, called ClassDojo, came under heavy scrutiny in early 2018 after a series of articles in the US and UK questioned its practice of gathering behavioral data and images from thousands of students and storing it all in an offshore location. ClassDojo promises "happier classrooms" through a platform that allows teachers to connect digitally to students and parents for the purposes of encouragement, transparency, and memory sharing. The app also helps teachers with organizational tasks and allows them to create digital portfolios of their students' work, and it has a game element for behavior—teachers can use it to award positive "dojo points" when children are respectful and negative ones when they misbehave. The company's website says it's used in 90 percent of schools in the US, but it's not clear exactly how many teachers use it, nor what they use it for, and some parents and education experts are nervous about its practices.

Similarly controversial tools seem to pop up every few months: many schools have started using internet filters and type trackers to detect when students' search behaviors suggest depression or suicidal ideation; the education company Pearson conducted a "social-psychological" experiment on thousands of unaware math and science students using its software, to see whether encouraging messages helped them solve problems; and one startup company, BrainCo, is raising millions in funding to create electronic headbands that will allow it to analyze students' brain data.

Chris Gilliard, a digital-education expert and English professor at Macomb Community College in Michigan, says that while the motives behind all these gadgets and programs can sound positive, the tools are still part of what he calls "surveillance capitalism," and we should be wary.

"The issue is that there are not a ton of laws that put [up] any guardrails, even on stuff that is used by kids," he told me on the phone. "In education technology, there's often a clause that says companies can use the data they collect to improve their product, and that's open to very broad interpretation."

It's rarely clear how long data is kept and who else might have access to it down the road. Gilliard is particularly worried about how this data might be used to make decisions about people in the future—say, when it comes time to apply for college, scholarships, and jobs. "We don't know, and we actually can't know, because a lot of times the companies don't even know," he said.

That point came into stark relief for me when I started reading about how Silicon Valley executives were shielding their own children from technology. Some keep their children away from screens altogether, including the very products they've made their money creating. "Never get high on your own supply" was the mantra told to *Guardian* journalist Alex Hern, who wrote in early 2018 about how the founders and CEOs at Facebook, Twitter, and other social-media networks don't use their own products the way the rest of us do, prioritizing privacy and control of their time. Even Apple CEO Tim Cook told a group of college students in London recently that while he didn't have a child of his own, he wouldn't allow his young nephew to use social media in his house.

The fact that these men feel the need to protect young people from their creations is telling, but the truth is that most regular people don't have that luxury. These tools have become so ubiquitous, it's nearly impossible to shield most kids from screens and what's on them, especially once they enter school. While abstaining is an option for some, it isn't for many, and it will likely become increasingly impractical going forward. Futurists like Jane McGonigal, director of game development and research at the Institute for the Future, which made the Face the

Future game, believe that it's important to acknowledge the dangers of any tool, but that we'll be better off if instead of hiding from those tools, we learn to harness them.

In 2016, McGonigal hosted a kickoff event in Boston for the Face the Future game. It took place just a few days after the election. I watched a remote stream of the event from New York as McGonigal addressed the crowd: "I couldn't have predicted how timely the topic of empathy would feel this week," she said. She put the tension in the room to work. We were all attempting to examine the same problem—the surprising election results—with different strategies, she explained. What if we tried to all get on the same page?

McGonigal led the audience in the room, and those of us watching from home, in a game. We each closed our eyes and imagined ourselves in a place we'd been, with a person we knew, doing a thing we'd done, but in a different combination than had ever occurred in real life. If we can do this, the thinking goes, we find that combination of people, places, and things more likely. I imagined myself riding a horse through a meadow in Sussex, England, with my husband. I've ridden a horse, I have been to a meadow in Sussex, and I have a husband, but these three things had never come together in this way in my real life. I was able to imagine it, though, by stitching together real memories of each individual piece: times I have ridden a horse, walked in a meadow in Sussex, and been close to my husband. This is known as counterfactual thinking. The theory is if we can train our minds to do this, it shouldn't be much of a stretch to train them to imagine someone else's experience.

"Empathy requires you to use your imagination in the same way," McGonigal said. "It requires you to get your brain to simulate something you have no personal, concrete experience with."

Studies show that triggering this type of empathy can lead to taking future action. But it doesn't happen without some work and a willingness to try imagining the unknown. In a room full of adults trying to do this, the mood was somewhat hesitant, somber, and quiet. But in a room full of students playing the Face the Future game, there was mostly enthusiasm and excitement. People tend to grow more skeptical as they get older, and many of us become more prone to overwhelm. But the next generation has already started answering some of the questions we are afraid to ask. When I described Face the Future to friends and colleagues, many struggled to wrap their minds around it or take it seriously. But the game itself hosted more than nine thousand students, eager to play.

CHAPTER 3
VR: THE EMPATHY MACHINE

Though the term *virtual reality* has been in the American lexicon since the 1980s, the concept existed long before, and it has evolved several times over the decades. For some it brings to mind the bright-red View-Master, a binocular-like stereoscope toy that allowed you to flip through images and almost feel like you were in the places you were seeing. Or it may conjure the book and/or movie *Ready Player One*, in which people in the not-too-distant future spend most of their time in a virtual world—either a dystopia or a utopia, depending on your perspective. Most people have been familiar with the idea of "being part of something you're watching," as my dad describes it, for almost as long as they can remember. The term *virtual reality* wasn't used until 1987, when Jaron Lanier, generally known as the father of VR, started building the first headsets most millennials would now recognize. But people were tinkering with ways to create immersive technology experiences for decades before that. In the 1950s, for example, filmmaker Morton Heilig created the Sensorama, an arcade-game-like booth that users could put their head inside to watch—and even smell and feel—a movie. Heilig patented the first head-mounted display in 1962, but the technology couldn't quite keep up with his dreams during his lifetime.

Nowadays, the hardware and software for these experiences has gotten a lot lighter, cheaper, and easier to come by. It's also become more varied. Even longtime experts tend to use the term *VR* as a catchall for a variety of immersive experiences. *Augmented reality* (AR) refers to computer-generated images put into your real-life field of vision through a technological device, often a smartphone's camera. Virtual reality is more of a pure immersive experience, though there are varieties within it, from simple 360-degree videos watched in a headset to full room-scale, three-dimensional VR. And *XR* (or cross reality) refers to an environment full of sensors and software that can be used to make VR or AR, and it creates a bridge between the physical and virtual worlds. Though a lot of people have still never tried on a VR headset, many people with smartphones are familiar with AR in game form. The most common iteration is probably the Instagram or Snapchat filters that add a mustache to your face or turn you into an animal, or the mobile game Pokémon GO that shows little animated Pokémon creatures in otherwise-banal places like parking lots and waiting rooms. In general, we're starting to get used to immersive technology as part of our lives.

My introduction to twenty-first-century XR happened in the summer of 2015. I was covering an event put on by the printer maker Epson for *Institutional Investor*, the financial magazine in New York where I worked at the time. Epson had rented out a big art gallery in Manhattan's Chelsea neighborhood and filled it with new products aimed at convincing investors that it was more than just a printer company.

"We are trying to change Epson's image," the company's president, Minoru Usui, told me through an interpreter, as we sat on stiff white chairs in a makeshift press room in the corner of the gallery. Epson had transformed the cement-floored and white-walled space into a showroom for a bunch of nontraditional new products: a machine that projected interactive images onto 3-D surfaces, robots operating a fabric printer, and a pair of smart glasses called Moverio.

While I was standing mesmerized by the fabric-printing robots, contemplating the future of employment for flesh-and-blood humans, an Epson employee called me over and urged me to try the smart glasses. I put them on, and I suddenly felt like I was in a high-tech spy movie. There was essentially a see-through computer screen framing everything I saw, and a controller allowed me to click on various tools. It was kind of like Google Glass, the ill-fated (perhaps before-their-time) smart glasses, but for mechanical work. The point of this simulation was to show how Moverio could be used in a manufacturing setting—a worker could theoretically test out different methods of building or fixing something virtually before actually doing it, or they could learn a new process by having the steps projected into their field of vision and simulated right in front of them.

It was a bit gimmicky, but it was one of my first inklings that immersive technology could be used in empathic ways. I knew it might not be the most altruistic example—its creators had put themselves in the shoes of workers to imagine what might be helpful for them to see in their field of vision while working, which could easily be exploited to push workers in harmful ways to be more efficient and productive. But creating a tool meant to be worn on someone's face and project images into their world requires a certain level of empathy, whether or not that's the goal. I started to wonder what it would look like if it were the goal.

I didn't know it at the time, but just a few months earlier, artist and filmmaker Chris Milk had stood onstage at the TED Conference in Vancouver and made the empathic potential of immersive technology more explicit than anyone had before.

In an effort to explain the demonstration he was about to give the audience to show off his latest project, Milk said: "What I was trying to do was to build the ultimate empathy machine."

Film, he explained, had always been a way to encourage the viewer's empathy for the person on the screen, and there were various ways to pull the audience further into the story using interactive elements. But all of these still required the screen to be essentially a window. "I want you through the window, on the other side, in the world," Milk said from the stage. So along with collaborators Gabo Arora, the Samsung corporation, and the United Nations, he had made *Clouds Over Sidra*, a VR film that put the viewer in the middle of the Syrian refugee crisis. Watching the film in a headset, turning from side to side to see the 360-degree footage, the viewer is meant to feel like they are sitting on the ground with a young girl named Sidra as she introduces herself. Next, they are surrounded by dozens of children as they file through a refugee camp lined with barbed wire.

"I think that we can change minds with this machine," Milk told the TED audience, and he said that he'd already started, by showing the film to a group of decision makers at the World Economic Forum in Davos. "They were affected by it," he said. "So we're going to make more."

At the time, many saw this as hyperbole. There were still few companies outside the gaming world that felt comfortable investing in VR content or hardware. But the idea of VR as an "empathy machine" has really taken hold in the world of advocacy and nonprofits over the past few years. Often quoting Milk, advocates for understanding refugees, Holocaust survivors, climate change, and more say they can change minds with just a few minutes in a headset. They only have to get people to sit down and put it on.

Going Virtual

Two summers later, my curiosity got the best of me and I played hooky from work to attend the VR for Change Summit, part of the Games for Change Festival at the New School in New York. I listened all day to presentations about how virtual reality could change the world, but I couldn't quite imagine how watching video in a headset would be that much different from watching it on a regular screen. I'd found myself close to tears often enough watching people—real and fictional—go through difficult things on the news and in movies and television. As I lined up to try a VR experience created by Planned Parenthood called *Across the Line*, I wondered what I'd feel with this headset on. Would the Planned Parenthood employees around me influence my experience? Would I have the "right" reaction to what I saw?

Soon enough it was my turn, and I donned the headset. It was bulky and weighed down on my nose and ears at first, but I quickly got used to it as my attention focused on what I was seeing and hearing. One of the first things that showed up in front of me was a note from the filmmakers: This film uses actual audio and video from protests across the United States to show the harassment health center staff and patients sometimes face.

Then I was inside an exam room. I seemed to be accompanying someone else who was there to see the doctor. A young-looking white woman with brown hair, in a long-sleeved white shirt and a puffy green vest, sat on the exam table and nodded solemnly as the doctor spoke. I had an urge to reach out and hold the young woman's hand as she answered questions and fiddled with her hands in her lap. At one point the doctor asked her if she was okay.

"No," she said after a beat.

"Are you unsure about your decision?" the doctor asked, and the woman shook her head. "Are you nervous about the procedure?"

"No, it was those people out there, the protesters."

The doctor came over, put her hand on the woman's shoulder, and apologized for what the woman had to go through to get there. Then the screen faded to black, and music began to play. More words popped up on the screen: 20 minutes earlier, outside a health center in Illinois. I appeared to be transported to the backseat of a car as the same young woman was being driven past rows of protesters on the way to the clinic. They held graphic signs and shouted things like, "All they're gonna do is kill your child!" One man in a reflective vest actually came up to the car, motioned for the woman to unroll her window, and begged her to avoid the clinic and let him take her to a different, "safer" place down the road. I felt my heart rate rise.

Then another message on the screen: All of the audio you are about to hear is real. It was recorded at protests throughout the United States.

Here we go, I thought, but I was surprised by what I saw next. The audio sounded real, but the surroundings—a street and sidewalk outside a clinic—were computer generated. A man in a green shirt stood a few feet away and yelled, "You're a whore! You're a whore! You're a little whore! How about not being a whore! Shame on you! Start closing your legs! Start having some respect for your body! Maybe your parents should have aborted you!" As I turned my head away from him, I saw a woman who appeared to be a clinic escort gesturing for me to follow her inside, but there was a line of protesters blocking the way. They seemed less menacing as computer-generated characters than they would have if they'd been real people. But knowing the voices were real did get to me. And as I listened to more and more of what these protesters had to say—"Why don't you close your legs and have some respect for your body?" "Maybe your parents should have aborted you!" on and on for more than two minutes—I thought there might be a reason they made this part cartoonish. Maybe it would have felt too real otherwise.

I felt a lot of things as I removed the headset. I was thankful that no one was looking at me expectantly, waiting for a reaction or review. I had to process the experience. But my first thought was that I was lucky. I had never been through that experience in real life. I felt like I could get closer to understanding what it was like now, but I couldn't help but wonder what a VR experience like this would be like for someone who didn't have the luxury of pretending. I also wondered whether an experience like this would really change someone's mind if they were truly opposed to Planned Parenthood's activities. I could think of a few people in my life who would have wanted to bail as soon as they saw a Planned Parenthood clinic referred to as a "health center" in the onscreen text. But maybe the point was that with VR, bailing out wasn't as easy as clicking a little ×. There was a social element to this as well—I could imagine wanting to prove I could stomach the experience, even if it boiled my blood.

Later that day at the summit, Dawn Laguens, Planned Parenthood's executive vice president and chief brand and experience officer, shared the story of a conservative antichoice lawmaker who donned a headset, viewed *Across the Line*, and left in a fury. He wasn't mad about Planned Parenthood, though; he was angry about the way the protesters treated the patients. This, she felt, was a win. And actually, this is the most common way that people are moved by these experiences—few report having immediate life-changing epiphanies, but many say they feel disturbed or inspired enough to start thinking about something a bit differently. It works for people who are already amenable to change as well, of course, but in sometimes surprising ways. Laguens also mentioned a man who had been a clinic escort for more than a decade and who left the *Across the Line* experience in tears, realizing that while he'd long since learned to block out the jeers and shouts and protesters, that wasn't possible for the women walking right beside him.

But can VR really do anything that other technology can't? There's some evidence to suggest that the answer is yes, but also that it might depend on what kind of person—and thinker—you already are before you put on the headset.

A 2018 report from the Tow Center for Digital Journalism found that stories experienced in VR "prompted a higher empathetic response than static photo/text treatments and a higher likelihood of participants to take 'political or social action' after viewing." The report defined "action" as either looking for more information, sharing the story, making a donation, or volunteering. Those who had more empathetic responses to the VR stories were also more likely to remember them, but a trustworthy narrator who stayed in regular contact throughout the experience was found to be vital. "Research showed that stories with one clear protagonist serving as a guide through the VR experience are consistently more enjoyable for users," the authors wrote. They also found that stories that were at least a little bit enjoyable had a bigger positive impact. And vitally, they found that no amount of immersion could counteract a user's lack of interest in, or overfamiliarity with, a subject.

This finding supports the idea that some people's predisposition might prevent them from becoming more empathetic toward certain other people, no matter how cool or innovative the technology is. A 2018 study published in the *Journal of Personality and Social Psychology* by Brian Lucas and Nour Kteily found that people's level of empathy seems to correlate with their position in society. In the study, more than three thousand subjects responded to eight surveys that described various people and scenarios. The researchers found that in a scenario in which a man was about to lose his work benefits, bringing harm to his family, participants had more empathy when the man was described as a factory worker than when he was described as an executive. It was as if the factory worker seemed more deserving. Rather than challenging biases, was the VR just amplifying them?

That possibility becomes more than a little disturbing when VR experiences depict something like racial or domestic violence, as they increasingly do.

1000 Cuts

Social scientist Courtney Cogburn is not a VR evangelist. A black woman with a background in academia, her goal was always to help people really understand racism—that it is much more than the KKK and white nationalists marching through the streets with tiki torches. She wanted to get beyond "hashtag activism"—the growing online social-justice movement—by educating people in a new way, in the hope that they would take that understanding a step further toward making change. Her target audience? Me. White liberals, who, she explained in a brightly lit New School classroom full of mostly white people one afternoon in June 2018, are "the group who is most likely to espouse beliefs of racial justice and equity but may not fully understand racial injustice, and they may not really understand how this infiltrates every part of people's lives, and has real implications for their mobility, their health, et cetera."

This was a concept I'd heard and thought about a lot, but I knew my understanding was still lacking, and that limited what I could do.

"How do we move more of us from superficial fluency in racial terminology . . . to more substantive knowledge and meaningful engagement around issues of race and racism?" she asked, to lots of staring eyes and a few nods. "Can immersive VR help improve our understanding of racial inequality?"

Cogburn admitted that she hadn't been sure at first and had started her project open to the idea that it might be a failure. When she cold-emailed Jeremy Bailenson, the VR expert at Stanford's Virtual Human Interaction Lab, she didn't even really know how VR worked. But Bailenson was intrigued by her idea, so they applied for funding and got to work on seeing whether stepping into the shoes of a young black man would do something more than interest and amuse white liberals.

"Can we do this in a meaningful way that doesn't turn racism into a game or entertainment?" Cogburn asked. "Can we do this in a way where people don't take off the headset and say, 'Now I know what it's like to be a black man'?" Instead, she wanted people to realize they really had no idea. "Empathy is important, but it is insufficient," she said. "You feeling bad doesn't do anything for the public good. Your actions do things for the public good."

As empiricists, Cogburn and Bailenson hoped that the mixture of data and personal narratives—some experienced by members of the creator team—would spur people to not only understand racism better but to want to do something to combat it.

I got to experience their project, *1000 Cut Journey*, that day. I slipped into a moderately heavy backpack, put a hot and already-sweaty headset over my eyes, and grabbed two long controllers—one for each hand. Then I stood in the dark for a few minutes as the machine booted up after a battery change. The first thing I noticed when I could see again was "my" hands. When I looked down at them, they were the hands of a computer-generated young black boy, whose name, I learned, was Michael Sterling. In the few seconds I had before moving through the narrative, I tried to imagine walking around embodied as someone else, someone with brown skin. It was still just imagining, don't get me wrong. But I had a visual to put with it now. I was about to have a whole lot more.

I stood and looked into a computer-generated mirror at the reflection of a black boy looking out at me and listened as a woman's voice welcomed me to the experience. The tall mirror was surrounded by an empty gray grid, which soon faded out and then back in around me, depicting a classroom. I was instructed to sit on the floor, which I did in real life, carefully, since I couldn't actually see my real surroundings. I looked up at holograms of several students and a teacher—real people edited into the computer-generated room. There were a few other kids on the floor with me, playing with Lego-like blocks. A white student started making mocking comments about the color of "my" skin. Suddenly without my control, "my" hand was throwing a block at the kid. Immediately, the teacher—who had been ignoring the young white boy's comments—stood up, looked down at me, and shouted at me, calling me "dangerous."

Feeling confused and frustrated, I stood up as the scene faded, and I found myself back in the empty space with the mirror, looking at the same boy, now a teenager. Once I got acclimated, I entered his room, where I walked around, careful not to walk outside the real-life confines of the carpeted exhibit booth. In VR, I was snooping through books, checking out a computer, posters on the wall, a basketball on the bed. Suddenly a phone began to ring, and using my controller I picked it up from a chair—it was a friend telling me to hurry up and come to the basketball game. Then suddenly I was downstairs, in an HGTV-worthy living room where "my" mother sat watching the news.

"You can't go out like that," she said as I picked up a hoodie that was draped over a chair. The friend who had called—a young white boy—stood impatiently at the door. "I just saw on TV that the cops are looking for someone," she said. "And you fit the description."

And indeed, almost as soon as we were out on the sidewalk, having ignored her warnings, I heard sirens. And almost before I could think about what to do next, a group of police officers surrounded me, yelling at me to get on my knees and put my hands up.

I looked up at the officers for a moment and felt a tension I hadn't ever felt before. When they left, having decided they had the wrong kid, the young white boy—my basketball teammate—called over, "I hope you're still ready for the game!" *You've got to be kidding,* I thought.

The next scene took place in a stylish office lobby, where I—now a much older version of Michael—handed over my résumé, clearly marked with the logos of Yale and Columbia. There was another man waiting to interview as well, a tall, conventionally attractive white man who made small talk with me about the stresses of interviewing. The prospective boss came out and made a beeline toward him, hand out, saying, "You must be our Yale graduate." This was when I noticed that I—the real Kaitlin—was angry and had been for a few minutes. My face was hot. I couldn't say anything—this wasn't real. The receptionist spoke up, but the boss said he was going to interview the white man first anyway. "You don't mind, do you?" he asked. I did. And when I found myself in the final scene, looking at myself in the mirror in a small white bathroom as the phone next to me began to ring, I knew what would happen when I answered it. No job.

And that was it. It was over. Two volunteers helped me out of the gear, and I fixed my hair, patted away the headset lines on my face, and went back out into the world. I felt dazed, but I had places to go and things to do, so I did.

This is the fundamental weakness of empathy VR, as even some of the most fervent supporters will tell you: in the end, you take the headset off and go back to your life. No matter how deeply you feel that you're embodying someone else for a while, it always comes to an end.

But I couldn't get it out of my head. I couldn't stop thinking about how it felt to look down and see brown-skinned hands, to hear the fear in a mother's voice as she worried about her son matching the description of someone the cops were looking for, to be frustrated and disappointed when the white boy's only response was to hope I was still ready to play basketball. A few hours later, I described the experience to some friends and, Cogburn's voice in my head, the impact started to come together: it wasn't that now I felt I knew what it was like to be a black man—it was more that I had a better appreciation for how *different* our experiences are.

In her talk earlier in the day, Cogburn had said that it shouldn't require the hundreds of thousands of dollars and hundreds of hours it took to create this VR project to get people to understand and care about racism. I already knew these things were happening on an intellectual level, and I'd worked to push against them in my own way. I was the target audience for this experience, and I also went into it open to empathy. What if I had been more skeptical to begin with? And what good does it do that I'm still thinking about it so long after the fact?

Making Convincing VR for Social Change

Imagine sitting in front of a computer and watching hours and hours of graphic raw video of an ongoing war. In 2004, that was Cathy Hackl's job in the video-production department at CNN. She was tasked with watching the raw video coming in from the Iraq War and flagging sensitive material so that the cable channel's local partners could warn viewers before they saw anything too offensive. In order to put this protection in place for the audience, Hackl had to sift through beheadings, the bodies of soldiers being dragged, anything that might set off cable's red flags. It was exhausting and traumatizing, and it took a toll on Hackl in a way that she hadn't anticipated.

"When you do that kind of job, you kind of turn your humanity switch off a little bit," she told me in 2017 for a story I wrote on this topic for the website Narratively. She became desensitized to these horrific images. Her ability to empathize took a backseat—it had to.

It was more than a decade before Hackl's empathy switch turned back on. She had been experimenting with 360-degree video, a technique that allows the viewer to feel surrounded by whatever they're watching, and at a tech conference she had the chance to try the HTC VIVE virtual-reality headset. Once inside the virtual world, she found herself in a solitary-confinement cell.

"Within a couple of minutes, I was completely claustrophobic," she said. The experience, called *6x9*, was created by the *Guardian*. In *6x9*, while wearing a VR headset, the viewer feels what it's like to be in solitary confinement in prison. They are transported to a tiny cell and are completely immersed, for a time, in that lonely, frightening atmosphere. "When I took the headset off, something clicked," said Hackl. "The humanity switch turned back on. I felt like I was actually walking in someone else's shoes."

Hackl said that after this experience, she felt sympathy for anyone who had to undergo solitary confinement in real life, but she also felt a call to action. She is now a consultant for some of the top virtual-reality and augmented-reality studios, making experiences with a social-impact focus. She is on the advisory council of Virtual Relief, a nonprofit that uses VR technology to help distract, entertain, and rehabilitate homebound seniors and hospital patients, and she considers herself an evangelist for the power of this technology.

While many people do have intense, moving experiences in VR, its proponents are still working to determine whether it can create change at scale. Much of the VR that people experience now is meant either for gaming or for showing off the bells and whistles of the technology. Since price tags can reach thousands of dollars, the companies and organizations making VR headsets and content still need to convince communities outside the tech world that the experience is worth it. In the past several years, as hardware has become cheaper and VR content has been created for broader audiences, the industry has made some progress.

"The people who are actually spending a lot of time crafting these stories and creating experiences are really moving the needle," Hackl told me. "I can turn off my phone or television, or take off a headset, but what really matters is what stays with you."

Planned Parenthood, which created the *Across the Line* VR experience I tried in New York, surveyed a group of viewers who were majority male, white, and liberal. The organization found that the group that saw *Across the Line* disapproved more strongly of some types of harassment after the experience than those who hadn't seen it. The experience was also linked to attitude changes in people who reported having moderate or slightly conservative political beliefs. No one magically became pro-choice, but some shifted to believing that protesters should not share anti-abortion views outside clinics. Some even came to "strongly agree" with the statement "I could support a woman who had an abortion (e.g., by driving her to an appointment) even if I didn't agree with her decision."

The technology seems to work against more subtle harassment and discrimination as well.

In 2016, London-based artist Andrew Daffy created a VR experience called HOLO-DOODLE that allowed two people to play

Pictionary together in a VR universe in which they were represented as pink monkeys. It was just for fun, but then people started telling Daffy that it made them feel less inhibited and better able to communicate with the person they played with. Daffy and his team decided to make some changes, and they debuted a new version of the game, called *I Am Robot*, the next year. This one allowed groups of people to don headsets and become genderless robots attending either a ballet recital, a cocktail gathering, or a dance party. The response from participants was surprising. Men in suits who swore they wouldn't dance became entirely different people in the genderless VR world; a woman with social anxiety who had struggled to enjoy herself at the conference put the headset on and, inhibitions gone, danced and laughed for the first time in days; another person said they felt comfortable being gender-free for the first time in their life in this VR atmosphere.

"We didn't make this to create social change. We just stumbled across it and thought, 'holy shit, this is the area we should be going into,'" Daffy said. "It's understandable to be worried about manipulation, and this kind of technology can seem so sci-fi and geeky and horrid. But there can also be such beauty."

Some people do undoubtedly experience beauty in VR experiences. Sometimes, actually, VR experiences can be *too* beautiful, as with *Melting Ice*, a film about environmental destruction, starring former vice president Al Gore, that left many viewers more amazed by the visual effects than the devastating facts about climate change. If the goal is creating empathy, these works have to deliver more than beautiful images and stories, but making them too real can also backfire. In addition to being potentially traumatizing, the experiences can verge on voyeuristic.

In March 2018, the International Committee of the Red Cross released a free AR app called *Enter the Room*, with the goal of "humanizing war." The user walks around in real life while holding their phone, and the setting in the app changes as the phone moves. They start in a colorful room, which then becomes dark and disheveled as the sounds of war are heard coming from outside. The room's occupant—clearly a young child—is never visible.

If VR experiences can trigger empathy in viewers, they can also trigger other feelings: stress, distress, overwhelm, exhaustion, anxiety, and, in cases where people with preexisting trauma may not have been adequately prepared, even symptoms of PTSD. There is a lot of debate in the psychology and tech communities about whether these reactions (apart from PTSD) are positive or negative. Some experts, including Chris Milk and Courtney Cogburn, have argued that it's necessary to be uncomfortable and upset as part of the journey toward empathy and eventually action. Others argue that being uncomfortable causes more people to simply turn away from an experience rather than having to continue to endure it.

Jeremy Bailenson, who has spent many years studying the impact of VR and has a positive view of the technology, once told CBS: "I think virtual reality is like uranium: It's this really powerful thing. It can heat homes and it can destroy nations. And it's all about how we use it."

"We want people to look at war not from their comfort zones or through the distance of a news article," Ariel Rubin, who led the creation of *Enter the Room*, said at the time. "We want to generate empathy towards the millions of people who face war every day, a reality which we, at ICRC, bear witness [to] far too often. Immersive tech like mobile AR can really remove those barriers to understanding and empathizing in a really powerful and immediate way."

The creators acknowledged that they couldn't literally make people feel what it's like to experience modern war. But they also stopped short of using the tech as a call to action. When a reporter for DMNews (a data and tech publication) asked Rubin if the point was to raise money for a cause, Rubin said no, the point was simply "awareness-raising." The experience made people agitated and upset, but there were no suggestions for what to do with that new energy. This is a problem with a lot of social-change VR. Yes, motivated people may leave such an experience and seek out a way to help or donate, but consider the environments most such experiences happen in: largely tech conferences, film festivals, and nonprofit events full of entertainment and distractions. This makes a VR experience's success hard to measure. Empathy is an emotion, and emotions are complex. Is it enough if, as people walk around after it's over, they're still thinking about it, as happened when I experienced *1000 Cuts*?

"We are really focusing on the use of VR as a tool for exploration," Cogburn said. "It is not a magic pill that's going to create high levels of empathy in all people around all issues. We don't know that yet, and we should be really thoughtful and careful about how we're using our technology."

Her caution is warranted, because some of these experiences overshoot in dramatic ways.

In 2015, an endeavor called the Elysium Project promised to change the way people grieve, creating personalized VR experiences that its creators claimed could "reunite" users with loved ones who had passed away. The plan was to allow people to inhabit a virtual environment with 3-D models of the deceased, through VR. The project garnered a ton of attention, but by 2016 it had put its plans on hold after receiving criticism and complaints. Though one of the creators, Steve Koutsouliotas, came up with the project after experiencing his own grief from the loss of his father and wishing to be able to spend time with him again, he later admitted to the *Washington Post* that he hadn't thought things all the way through. He needed to go back to the drawing board to make an experience "people will not only love but won't be offended or terrified by."

A similar approach has been used to more successful—though still controversial—effect in Holocaust education. Several projects aim to capture the stories of Holocaust survivors and build immersive experiences around them, in hopes of ensuring that they won't be forgotten. In *The Last Goodbye*, produced by the USC Shoah Foundation, viewers travel with eighty-five-year-old Pinchas Gutter back to Majdanek, a former Nazi concentration camp where he was imprisoned at age eleven. The creators gathered thousands of 3-D images of the camp, and they filmed Gutter telling his story with 360-degree cameras against a greenscreen backdrop on location. They tied everything together to make the person experiencing *The Last Goodbye* feel as if they were standing with Gutter in that setting while hearing the gut-wrenching story from the man himself.

The project debuted to great acclaim at the Tribeca Film Festival in 2017, where attendees could experience it at room scale. It's also still available for anyone with a smartphone on the VR app Within.

As high minded as these experiences are meant to be, to some they still feel like invitations to become tourists in others' lives. Many in the disability-rights community, for example, express concern about people being able to simply play in their realities through VR simulations that can easily be turned off. Disability simulations are often used in the medical context as a teaching tool for clinicians. But many are also available to the public, allowing people to simulate cataracts, visual migraines, and mental illnesses like schizophrenia.

"While it's intended to increase understanding, it could very well instead evoke some kind of pity, or a feeling of being inspired by people with disabilities for 'overcoming,'" Emily Ladau, a writer and disability-rights activist, told me. The problem with simulation, she said, is that even though the goal is to point people in the direction of understanding someone else's humanity, there's always the risk of taking that humanity away by reducing constant, everyday obstacles to momentary inconveniences. She recommends including people with disabilities in the creation of simulations and in events where nondisabled people will be experiencing them.

"When you do a simulation, you're coming to it with your own biases, and if you don't have someone there to help who actually knows what the experience is like, that's where the disconnect starts happening," she said. "It's a delicate balance."

Homelessness simulators, like Stanford's *Becoming Homeless: A Human Experience*, face a similar problem. They are essentially VR games that put viewers through the paces of living life on the street. Though some research has shown that many people emerge from simulation experiences with a greater appreciation for how others live, some negative reactions seem more visceral. When in 2017 a group of Australian CEOs participated in the CEO Sleepout, in which they spent a night sleeping outside on cardboard boxes and also experienced a VR homelessness simulator, many critics responded that the whole idea was "dystopian" and "out of touch." They might have been right. Some research has suggested that people who have lived through a particular experience can sometimes be less empathetic toward others going through the same thing.

"The very concept of empathy creation through VR is an [o]thering process," journalist Inkoo Kang wrote in Slate in 2017. "So-and-so's experiences are so vastly different from yours, it's presumed, that you can only understand their situation if you step into their shoes."

This statement made me pause when I read it. I had always felt that I couldn't truly understand *anyone's* life unless I tried to walk in their shoes, whether through listening to their story or experiencing it in some other way.

But I realized VR creators aren't making experiences about everyone. The ones that get made, and especially those that receive the biggest headlines, are about people and places that are most traditionally marginalized; most of the people making and viewing them are not from those communities. Though there has been diverse representation among VR developers, just as with the advent of other new technologies, the distribution of money and power has tended to elevate white male developers over their peers who are women and people of color, naturally limiting the perspectives and voices depicted. This fact has been highlighted as one of the reasons for Facebook CEO Mark Zuckerberg's foray into empathy-building VR after Hurricane Maria devastated Puerto Rico. The video, in which smiling cartoon avatars of Zuckerberg and Rachel Rubin Franklin, head of social VR, gave a virtual tour of the destruction, was poorly received, with some critics suggesting that if the production team had been less homogenous, the racial and political context of the disaster would have been clearer and Zuckerberg might have realized the extent to which the stunt would come across as exploitative.

"Hot topics can be distracting," said Courtney Cogburn, the creator of *1000 Cuts*. "It's important for us to know our intent . . . also acknowledging that you can do damage to the community you're trying to represent. It's not just a story."

Sharpening the Tool of VR

In the spring and summer of 2018, while immigrant families were being separated at the US-Mexico border and children were being held without their parents, toys, or adequate medical care in detention centers, visitors to Washington, DC—and, presumably, the politicians who worked there—had the opportunity to experience one immigration story for themselves. Alejandro González Iñárritu's Oscar-winning VR experience *Carne y Arena* starts before the headset is even on, with participants entering a cold room reminiscent of a detention-center holding cell and being asked to rid themselves of their belongings. They next walk into a sandy room to don the hardware. The VR experience takes place in the Sonoran Desert, with migrants, immigration officers, and even mirages all around. The experience has been described as literal in some ways, and conceptual in others—the video has a dreamy quality, and as you walk around, you might pass through another virtual character and see a representation of their beating heart in the middle of the screen as you do so. But at the same time, the sandy landscape feels truly barren.

The experience is undoubtedly moving, but Ben Davis, the national art critic at Artnet, pointed out that the unreality of the experience was extremely difficult to ignore. "As vivid as the experience gets, you are also at all times keenly aware that the very same basic set-up lets you experience, say, being a Space Marine shooting demons in the head or scaling a 200-foot-tall amethyst octopus," he wrote.

Davis admitted that the tech was impressive, but he was not convinced of the empathic capabilities. He referenced a 1924 book of graphic photos called *War Against War!* by Ernst Friedrich, which became a bestseller in part on the basis of its ability to force people to acknowledge the horrors of World War I. Many people who saw it, though, were simply disgusted by the pictures of the carnage. Overall, Davis wrote of *Carne y Arena*: "Its existence is positive." What he would change is how it, and experiences like it, are framed.

"What I lament is that *Carne y Arena* puts so many eggs in the basket of creating empathy, since its power so clearly depends on a foundation of pre-existing sympathy," he wrote. "And what I wish—especially now that Iñárritu's work is directly inserting itself into the political conversation—is that it was connected to more of a call to action than just daring Trump to see it."

Even Chris Milk, who popularized the idea of VR as an empathy machine, may not have meant it literally. As Kamal Sinclair, a film producer and digital-media critic, wrote in 2017 as part of a research project called Making a New Reality, Milk told her that his goal was to encourage people to see VR as more than a toy, but he never meant to suggest that the technology or the empathy it evokes could solve problems on their own. "He assumed the audience would consider VR as just a tool for those working to further connection between traditionally divided people," Sinclair wrote.

The idea of technology as a tool is prominent among both critics and evangelists. Too often, it is used to excuse negligent development and design. It's true that creations reflect their creators, and as long as people are making technology, it will be imperfect. But that doesn't have to mean it's not useful. It just means we have to get comfortable with making the tough decisions that will make it worthwhile.

CHAPTER 4
FEELING THE NEWS

I look around the tiny cinder-block cell and see only a toilet, a heavy metal door, and a cot-like bed. As I'm adjusting to the low light and claustrophobic space, I hear a voice, and suddenly I'm not alone in the room. There's a man in red basketball shorts and a red T-shirt sitting on the bed, telling me about his time in solitary confinement. He seems out of place but at the same time comfortable. This was the only world he knew for years, he says, and it's been a struggle to adjust to the wider one since he left.

I can't lift the shade or open the door or ask this man any questions, because this isn't my reality but a virtual one. The cinder-block walls flash facts about the use of solitary confinement in US prisons, as Kenneth Moore, who spent eight years in this tiny cell in Maine State Prison on charges of aggravated assault, burglary, and theft, talks about how he self-harmed during that time and how he felt it slowly drive him insane. I'm not exactly experiencing what it was like for him—I forget for only a moment that I could take the headset off if I wanted to. But no matter how many words I've read about the horrors of solitary confinement, there's something about hearing the story from a person who's experienced it, in the place where they experienced it—even virtually—that makes it different. As a person who prides herself on her ability to empathize—and especially as a journalist—I'm a bit embarrassed to admit it, but this feels more real.

Nonny de la Peña and the documentarians at PBS *Frontline* created this VR experience, called *After Solitary*, with a purely journalistic mission. De la Peña spent twenty years as a correspondent for *Newsweek* and then as an independent documentarian, always wishing for a better way to get viewers to feel a "fully embodied connection" to the stories she told. If viewers could feel they were really *in* the stories, she thought, they might understand them better. Her first experiment was a collaboration with the artist Peggy Weil in 2007. They created a version of the prison at Guantanamo Bay called *Gone Gitmo* in the online virtual world Second Life. The response was overwhelmingly positive. Her hypothesis seemed to be correct. "After we made that, I had a big realization that the current technology could be used for all kinds of journalism," she told me. She secured a small grant from the MacArthur Foundation, which ultimately helped her shape the concept of immersive journalism. She's now considered by many to be the "godmother of virtual reality," but not all of her peers were enthusiastic at the beginning.

Her first immersive journalism VR piece after *Gone Gitmo* was *Hunger in LA*. It simulates the experience of standing in line outside a Los Angeles food bank when suddenly a diabetic man in line falls to the ground, suffering from a seizure. The piece uses audio from a real incident, played over animation. The animation creates a distance between the viewer and the characters, but the raw audio is intense. "*Hunger* was not an easy piece to get made, nor to get interest in from my journalism colleagues," de la Peña told me. Some saw it as a gimmick; others were worried about the ethics of manipulating sound and images in this way. She went on to create a string of poignant pieces, including *Use of Force*, which depicts the beating of a man at a border crossing, and *Project Syria*, where the user is in Aleppo as an attack unfolds.

The journalism industry has a reputation for failing to keep up with the times. It notoriously struggled to adjust to the internet age and is, in fact, still struggling to find a sustainable way of monetizing itself now that it's accepted the conditions of twenty-first-century storytelling. Meanwhile, pernicious trends have crept in: "fake news" in the sense of misleading clickbait headlines and "fake news" in the actual propaganda sense have both been able to propagate freely, while writers and editors toil away in underfunded newsrooms or, more frequently, as underpaid freelancers in coworking spaces and on living-room couches. Seeking to maintain trust and prestige, the titans of the industry—if we can still call them that—have kept their eyes on the ever-precious prize of objectivity.

A 2016 Gallup poll showed that people trust the media even less than they trust Congress, which has never been popular. This isn't exactly a new problem, but it's gotten worse in the era of "fake news." I have a relative who trusts Infowars and YouTube more than CNN, the *New York Times*, or any other established news organization, not just because of a general desire to be contrary, but because she feels that Infowars and YouTube understand her in a way that the "mainstream media" doesn't. Before being banned by mainstream social-networking venues like Facebook and YouTube, Alex Jones of Infowars spent years building a very specific audience that shares a lot of the same fears and desires about immigration and government control, and he has enough loyal followers to keep his videos coming on his own website, despite being "deplatformed" in other locations on the social web. In a counter-intuitive way, he accomplished this by empathizing with his audience. When he screams into his microphone, he's screaming not just points of information but also points of emotion. He and his more mainstream peers like Rush Limbaugh and Tucker Carlson often address their audiences directly. They acknowledge and validate the fears of their listeners and viewers. That's powerful, even if what they say turns out to be misleading or exaggerated, and especially when it's incendiary. And at the same time, the mainstream media has made some pretty monumental mistakes, from failing to recognize the economic and cultural woes of a huge swath of the American population not living on the coasts to helping fuel the fire of divisive rhetoric and behavior that makes good headlines.

At a time when the public's trust in the media seems more tenuous than ever, many journalists feel it's especially important to make sure that they don't even allow for the suggestion that they (and I—a member of the media who might find myself using this technology at some point) might be manipulating our audiences. But shying away from new technology because it doesn't fit existing norms can backfire, making reporters seem out of touch.

In 2017, *After Solitary* won the Excellence in Immersive Storytelling award from the Online Journalism Awards. All signs point to immersive experiences as the future of journalism—or, at least, *a* future. And yet, they break all the rules.

But objectivity at the expense of empathy, rather than saving us, may have pushed us to this precarious point even faster.

VR will not be a panacea, but it might help journalists get people more invested in their stories.

And that's where immersion comes in. Much of the technology this industry has shunned, for fear that it is too much like entertainment or gaming, actually has the ability to connect people more closely with our stories and help them feel understood in ways we dream about doing with words alone. Caution about diving into this new world of immersive journalism is understandable, but it will ultimately be self-defeating if we aren't careful. Trust in journalists and the media sank to a new low in 2016, and in 2018 still less than half of those polled by Gallup said they trusted the media to report the news accurately. At the same time, calls have grown louder for more empathy in reporting about people who are marginalized or who feel left behind by our country's politics. Now, as the technology for VR becomes more available and affordable, this seems like the right time to take that risk. And increasingly, traditional news creators are asking: What do we have to lose?

VR News Pioneers

When Hurricane Katrina made landfall in August 2005, it devastated dozens of towns and displaced more than a million people. Images of the destruction flashed across screens and front pages for weeks as rescue and cleanup efforts wore on, and it was the first time I ever heard the phrase "compassion fatigue." Sometimes things are just so bad, so overwhelming, that our psyches protect us from feeling the pain of others, and we go numb. This phenomenon is not unique to hurricanes, but the storm came at a pivotal time in the evolution of journalism and technology, creating a special opportunity.

Visitors to MSNBC.com during fall 2005 could do more than view photos and videos—they could virtually stand in the middle of the destruction, surrounded by debris, sand, water, and the remnants of cars and homes. Suddenly it felt like being there. To viewers who lived in other parts of the country or the world, the people affected by this disaster were no longer anonymous strangers providing sound bites—anyone with an internet connection could step briefly into their shoes, thanks to the first journalistic use of 360-degree video. The project, called *Rising from Ruin: Two Towns Rebuild After Katrina*, chronicled the rebuilding efforts in Bay St. Louis and Waveland, two towns on the Mississippi coast. In addition to daily dispatches in blog and photo form, the project provided videos that gave viewers the ability to look around—nearly all the way around—at the wreckage. The piece won the National Press Club Online Journalism Award for Best Journalism Site in 2006, and it helped inspire an entirely new genre of news that did more than inform—it triggered and encouraged empathy.

The videos, which are unfortunately no longer available online, were created with the help of a "human tripod," reporter Ashley Wells. He wore about $15,000 worth of gear on his body, including a spherical digital video camera with six lenses mounted on a skydiving helmet, plus two 40 GB hard drives for the camera in a backpack, and he carried a laptop and a separate camera to record audio. Since then, things have gotten a bit less cumbersome. The equipment is still expensive, but it's not quite as heavy. It's become so mobile, in fact, that it can go places many people may never go themselves.

To make *The Displaced*, a 360-degree perspective-taking documentary, videographers from the *New York Times Magazine* traveled around the world to document the lives of refugee children displaced by war and persecution. It would be heart-rending to read or watch them tell their stories. But there's something about just being with them, even virtually, as they go about their day, that triggers empathy in a different way. Feeling as if I'm standing on the damaged roof of an old building as children scurry around me, and the sensation that I'm in the canoe that a child is paddling, or in a crumbling classroom with them, makes me feel connected in a way that lends itself to a new level of understanding. Being able to look around and see what they see, choosing which way to turn my head without being directed, suggests a reality that just doesn't come through in other media.

When it released the project in 2015, the *Times* was explicit about its hope of inspiring empathy through the use of this new technology: "The power of VR is that it gives the viewer a unique sense of empathic connection to people and events," editor Jake Silverstein said at the time.

Other news outlets, such as VICE, ABC News, and even the *Wall Street Journal*, have followed suit, producing long- and short-form VR experiences. *Frontline*'s award-winning *After Solitary* also gives the medium a sense of credibility it didn't have before. But VR is still largely an afterthought at many publications—something cool and new but not fully understood. And while it passes the objectivity test of many editors and distributors, it raises many of its own issues.

Ethical Empathy in Journalism

Journalism's traditional way of negotiating necessary breaches in objectivity is to be as transparent as possible. That's why you'll sometimes see parentheticals in which a journalist reveals that they have some personal connection to the story, or a note at the bottom of a story acknowledging that one of the subjects has an ownership stake in the publication. This is done not to suggest that the reporter can't be trusted, but to remind you that they're human, while still trying to be clear about the conflicts that being human can create.

But how do you do this when the reader or viewer is *inside* the story? And an entire immersion experience is based on gaining enough of a person's trust to effectively manipulate their emotions?

While creating *After Solitary*, de la Peña and her team wanted viewers to be able to feel like they were in the solitary-confinement cell with Kenneth Moore. But they filmed him after he'd gotten out of jail, and they couldn't ask him to put himself back in that cell for filming.

"It was an interesting moment," de la Peña said.

This conundrum could have been solved by using animation. Moore would have been placed in front of a green screen and hooked up to a bunch of sensors that would turn him into a cartoon version of himself, much like what happens to create the CGI we see in movies. Or the digital animation could have simply been made independently, based on video, as happened with *Hunger* and several of de la Peña's other projects, including Planned Parenthood's *Across the Line*. But the technology for holograms had recently evolved, and the team felt this would be more realistic. So they filmed Moore speaking and put him in the cell as a hologram that would interact with the viewer. Think the Princess Leia hologram in *Star Wars: A New Hope*, but with better pixel quality.

Still, there was another problem: What should he wear?

For the full empathetic experience, a viewer might expect Moore to be in his prison uniform. But that posed an ethical issue: it might suggest that he had actually been filmed while still imprisoned. That may seem like a small thing, but journalists avoid inaccurate inferences in order to maintain as much objectivity and integrity as possible. If a documentarian misleads you about where a person was when they were filmed, the thinking goes, how else might they manipulate you?

So in *After Solitary*, Moore wears his regular civilian clothes—basketball shorts, T-shirt—because that's what he wore when he was interviewed. It also provides some important story context, making it clear from the beginning that he's telling a story after the fact, in a virtual environment meant to mimic his previous surroundings. It's immersive, it's ethical, and it works.

"There are still some things we have to figure out. We're still cutting new ground," de la Peña told me. "But if a traditional and careful organization like *Frontline* can be satisfied with the content we're producing, I would suggest that many of the issues raised are nonsensical."

The threats of manipulation and subjectivity are more easily dismissed when it comes to advertising and nonprofit outreach. But in journalism it's important to evoke empathy without coming across as if you're forcefully extracting it.

Some immersive experiences toe this line more precariously than others, and some defy categorization.

Clouds Over Sidra, the 2015 VR film about the Syrian refugee crisis, puts the viewer right in the middle of a refugee camp full of children. Gabo Arora, who made the film with Chris Milk in partnership with the UN and Samsung, has explained that one scene was fabricated. According to "The Ethics of Immersive Journalism: A Rhetorical Analysis of News Storytelling with Virtual Reality Technology," a paper recently published by Hollis Kool of Stanford University in the university's science-and-technology journal, Arora gathered about a hundred children and staged a scene with them running up to the camera in order to "make the viewer feel like a member of [the group] rather than a distant spectacle." Hollis wrote, "It was a smart but deceitful empathy-generating manipulation to give a false sense of humanism."

In the midst of the experience, if you didn't know the scene was staged, you might not even realize it. And ultimately, it's up to you whether you care. Does knowing that one element was faked diminish your trust in the rest of the piece? Could it be fake if the feeling it evoked in you was real?

There's also a more obvious omission: in most of these experiences, the journalists and cameras are absent.

"With more moving parts . . . storytelling becomes more complex and also more ethically weighty," Hollis wrote. "The invisibility of the journalist in VR can be a dangerous illusion in the consumption of media when viewers begin to analyze, relate to, and act on the stories they consume." Removing the journalist and the camera from the experience, she said, "is ethically precarious because behind the convincingly present sensation of a VR experience is the orchestrating journalist. In the construction of *Clouds Over Sidra*, the producers had major regulatory power about what aspects of the refugee camp the viewer sees, hears, and experiences."

That sounds kind of menacing. But is it really that different from any other media we consume? There are always editors and producers behind the scenes. It's part of the cultural contract (or at least it's supposed to be) that we take journalists at their word even when we can't see them. Some experts worry that one misstep with VR could set off a landslide that crumbles immersive media's ethical credibility for good. This fear is understandable, but it gives consumers too little credit. People's responses to VR experiences suggest that most understand that what they're seeing is, by necessity, the product of a certain amount of editorial magic.

New Dimensions in Testimony is, depending on your perspective, an oral-history project, a documentary project, a journalism project, a neat way to showcase hologram technology, or some mixture of all of the above. Created by the University of Southern California Institute for Creative Technologies and the USC Shoah Foundation, it records and displays testimonies from Holocaust survivors. Working with interactive storytelling firm Conscience Display, the project uses technology pioneered by USC's researchers to capture each survivor's face and body as they speak so they can be projected onto high-fidelity screens. Not only can you look at a person who feels so close and real you want to reach out and touch them, you can speak to them—and they will speak back. The project uses natural-language-processing technology to allow viewers to ask questions about the survivors' experiences and get answers.

Is any of this journalism? What if the survivors in *New Dimensions in Testimony* were put—virtually—into concentration camps, so that you spoke to them while they walked through the sites of their torment? Would that be descriptive, or excessive? At what point would the experience cross over from encounter to exploitation, your empathy coming at the expense of their retraumatization? Social-justice activists have termed this phenomenon *trauma porn*, a spectacle that makes viewers feel good about themselves while giving no benefit—and at times perpetuating harm—to the individuals and communities being depicted.

This is the piece that most bothers me as a journalist. I want to explain things to people and make them feel a connection, but I don't want to engender empathy at the expense of the truth or the humanity of those depicted. I've talked to many colleagues who agree. "I always want people to empathize, but the idea that VR is the empathy machine has been overused," said Cassandra Herman, a documentary director and producer. "It's become an accepted concept that in some ways suggests people don't have to work as hard to understand things."

This concern calls to mind the broader problems facing VR. At the VR for Change Summit in New York in 2017, the makers of the hit augmented-reality game That Dragon, Cancer, questioned the goals of the genre they'd helped create. Their game asks players to take on the life of a parent (based on the game creators) whose child is dying; Amy Green emphasized that while it was nice to hear from so many people who felt moved by the game, none of them could really know what it was like to lose a child to cancer unless they experienced it themselves. What, Green wondered, should the player *do* with the empathy they feel?

In journalism, the answer to this is often beside the point—and out of the creator's hands. People want information from journalists, not directions for how to feel or what to do.

The truth is that it might not matter how much journalists wring their hands about this question. Research shows that consumers of VR journalism are more plugged in to the feelings such an experience might leave them with than the journalistic details.

In July 2017, the Google News Lab completed a study to see how VR could be useful in journalism. The biggest finding was that viewers remember the VR experiences that leave them with powerful emotions. This is part of the challenge of combating misinformation—it's far easier to recall how a news story made us feel than the facts it actually presented. But it's also validation that VR journalism, when done right, can be a powerful tool for empathy. Rather than simply choosing to pull a viewer's heartstrings with an immersive story over presenting facts, the real skill in VR journalism is the ability to draw the viewer in with a narrative that conveys a few meticulously selected facts. The fact that there are thousands of displaced children around the world who are fending for themselves, for example, or that solitary confinement can have a deep effect on a person's life even after they're released. People just can't retain much data when immersed in a 360-degree VR world.

It's a problem of FOMO—the fear of missing out. Katy Newton and Karin Soukup, a filmmaker and designer who have written a guide to VR storytelling, have conducted research showing that people are sometimes overwhelmed by 360-degree video: they don't know where to look, and they worry that while they're gazing in one direction, they might miss something important happening in another. I've experienced VR FOMO while watching the 360-degree video clips that the *New York Times* used to send out in its daily email newsletters. The image often got pixelated when I clicked and dragged to move within the scene, and the onscreen text was often visible only from certain positions, so I worried I was missing important context while looking around. Some *New York Times* commenters expressed similar frustrations, including the common argument that the experience often feels too "voyeuristic."

Newton and Soukup's research showed that having so many elements to focus on in a VR experience can stress out participants as they try to take everything in. The researchers noted that "Looking *is* doing, and it requires a lot of work from the audience." Part of the point of VR should be to cut down on "information clutter." Newton and Soukup's findings mirrored those of Google: the best sensory experiences are bigger on empathy and lower on data. "Perhaps being present and retaining story details are fundamentally at odds," they wrote.

But that doesn't always have to be the case. De la Peña's *Use of Force* is one example of how VR can go well. The viewer watches through a fence, surrounded by other onlookers shouting and crying, as Anastasio Hernández Rojas is beaten to death for trying to cross the border between the US and Mexico. There's little context to the story, but the viewer comes away with an intense experience and a desire to know more. The basic details are clear: this is a border crossing, someone is being brutalized, there's a sense of injustice. There isn't time or room to go through every detail within the experience, but the feeling the viewer is left with is likely to lead them to watch or read more. And unlike social-change VR, this is a logical stopping point for journalism. It's true to the mission of most journalistic organizations—informing and encouraging people to ask more questions without proselytizing.

The New Normal

These VR stories won't reach everyone who experiences them, and for some people they will be too intense. And it's true that, unlike with a long article or a documentary, people don't tend to come away from these pieces remembering facts and figures—they remember feelings. But those feelings can lead them to new perspectives, which is a sign of good journalism.

In the summer of 2017, Robert Hernandez drove from Los Angeles to the US-Mexico border to take a 360-degree video of a sixty-five-foot mural of a toddler positioned to look like he was peering over the border wall. The mural, created by the French artist JR, was an arresting depiction of the tense divide over immigration in America, and Hernandez wanted to document it in a way that would make the viewer feel its towering presence, even from afar. He started working in 360-degree video about eight years ago after meeting Nonny de la Peña.

"I remember her talking about VR, and I was thinking, man, you're crazy, it's been hyped forever and it's never going to scale," he told me. "She just proved us wrong." Hernandez now teaches a class at the USC Annenberg School for Communication and Journalism, called JOVRNALISM. His students partnered with the *Times*'s 360-degree-video team to create VR experiences documenting Donald Trump's inauguration and the Women's March on Washington in 2017. The student team also created immersive "postcards"—more a snapshot of an event than a story—that NPR shared on social media. It was the first time the public-radio giant had come close to publishing 360-degree news.

One day in fall 2016, the class was working on a project with ProPublica, the nonprofit investigative journalism organization, with the goal of using VR to get people to pay more attention to and prepare for impending disasters. This was the opposite of "disaster porn." It was service journalism about getting the people in the path of a storm to really take it seriously, by putting them through the experience of a virtual storm surge. The trick was to do it without fabricating a story.

"We were brainstorming, and the students started to say things like, 'Let's make the lightning flash and the wind blow and the roof rip off the house while the viewer is standing in it.' I stopped and reminded them: 'That's no longer journalism, you're hypothesizing a situation,'" Hernandez said. "'Let's stick to the facts.' We boiled it down to: What is a storm surge? And what does it mean when a wall of water is coming at you? There's nothing wrong with hypothesizing, and someone else can do that, but our goal is to inform with facts the best we can."

The result was not lacking in emotion. It's hard not to feel something when you see a ten-foot wall of water coming straight up to a house. You get the sense of scale, and it sends a message.

"We don't let the water hit the house, because we don't know how it would react, if it would flood, if the house would crumble. That's not our job. Our job was to give you a sense of scale, and we did that," Hernandez said.

So where does empathy come in with a project like this? It's in the impetus for the project itself—empathizing with people who need a better visualization of the danger to themselves and their homes in a flood—and it's in the hint of fear the viewer feels as the water rises, knowing that they can look away now but that in a real emergency they could not.

Hernandez doesn't think about empathy quite so explicitly when he makes VR experiences with his students, but he admits its role is impossible to deny.

"Let's not be foolish and believe that because you did a VR experience you know what it's like to be a girl in a refugee camp, but I do believe it gets you a bit closer," he said. "It helps you get through the noise. VR gives this incredible opportunity that allows you to hold presence with people [and experiences] you might not have access to."

Now Hernandez finds himself in the position of teaching others—both USC students and fellow professional journalists—how augmented reality and VR can enhance their journalism.

"Folks in the industry who didn't believe me all of a sudden are asking questions, asking for advice, experimenting on their own," Hernandez said. "It's constantly evolving and changing, and it's an opportunity for us to advance our storytelling and the medium."

The *New York Times* giving out over a million Google Cardboards to subscribers in 2015 so they could experience *The Displaced* was a turning point. But Hernandez sees in AR and VR even more of a democratizing effect for newsrooms. The technology has now reached the point that you don't have to be the *New York Times* to create this kind of immersive experience. Hernandez's specialty is looking for emerging technology right when it becomes accessible to storytellers. He's working now to find more efficient ways to share AR and VR with the industry and, he hopes, force it to evolve.

"We're not supposed to use the word *inevitable*, but I do," said Hernandez. "We're not going back."

CHAPTER 5
EMPATHY AT WORK

In 2016, the Equal Employment Opportunity Commission released a report showing that a third of the ninety thousand complaints it had handled in the previous year were related to harassment in the workplace, with 45 percent involving harassment on the basis of sex and 34 percent involving harassment on the basis of race. Fifteen percent of cases involved age discrimination, and 20 percent involved harassment on the basis of a disability. And those were just the reported incidents.

Whether outright harassment and assault or small daily acts of condescension, these types of incidents take a toll, and they affect employee morale and productivity. I've experienced a level of this myself.

In fall 2017, while working at a nonprofit, I attended an event about the unique challenges and opportunities faced by women in the business and legal industries. The #TimesUp movement, which focuses on the harassment and abuse of women in the workplace, was just beginning, and the event was packed. I was covering for a male coworker, who unexpectedly showed up just before the keynote speech began. I commented on his nice coat.

"Speaking of sartorial choices," he said, opening the coat and pointing to the crotch of his pants. "Check out these buttons!"

I gaped. My first thought was that he was just irredeemably awkward in social situations. There was nothing special about the buttons, at least as far as I could tell in one inadvertent glance, except that they existed in place of a zipper. We were at work. At an event about women's empowerment. How could *anyone* explain this one? The keynote started before I had to come up with some kind of response, but the coworker followed me to the table where I had stationed myself and my notebook.

"Let's hope no one says anything . . . bad," he said, and then he winked. "You know, considering the climate right now . . ."

It had been about a week since the news broke of multiple allegations of sexual assault and career destruction against Hollywood producer Harvey Weinstein, and more big-name men in the industry were beginning to get their comeuppances as well. We'd been talking pretty openly about the issue in my office. Some of the men were showing shock, but most of the women were simply angry. This particular coworker hadn't really participated in those conversations, so I was a little surprised at how brazen he was being. I decided not to respond—I had work to do. Saying he had to go, my coworker rested his hand on the small of my back, thanked me for covering the event, then slipped out.

These were small interactions, probably unnoticed by anyone else in the room. I had been shown much worse than a buttoned-up fly without my consent (though not at work). And I knew that his attitude about this event didn't matter in the scheme of things—there was still a panel of accomplished women at the front of the room sharing their experiences and advice, and he couldn't take that away. I knew I was good at my job, and that I wasn't covering this event for his benefit but for the benefit of myself and our organization. Still, his effort to minimize the issue, condescend to me, and invade my personal space all at once left me feeling uncomfortable and annoyed, when I'd just been trying to do my job. I was able to brush it off and move on—it was only one of dozens of similar experiences I'd have that month, of hundreds I'd have that year. But it wasn't as easy for my younger coworker, who later said she had been surreptitiously photographed by him from behind while working the event. We both reported him to Human Resources and were told it would be handled with discretion. The only difference we noticed was that he spoke to us less in the halls. I left the job a few months later.

As the #TimesUp movement has grown, it's become hard to ignore the fact that a huge number of women experience interactions somewhere on the spectrum of harassment and assault at work, from sexist comments to nonconsensual touching to rape. This issue is not new, but the outcry surrounding it, and the call for empathy for the victims, has reached a new pitch. But what about stopping behavior like this before it starts? Many organizations require employees to go through some kind of educational training on sexual harassment or diversity and inclusion, but the problem persists. Could empathy training be the answer?

A growing number of influential organizations think so. In fact, companies like Microsoft, Amazon, Fidelity, and the Bill & Melinda Gates Foundation are banking on the idea that not only will empathy training keep employees from behaving badly, it will make them more motivated and productive too. Empathy is getting so big in the business world that there are at least two massive indices—one created by the *Harvard Business Review* and one made by UK company The Empathy Business—that rank companies on their empathy. Facebook, Google, LinkedIn, and Netflix regularly top the lists. It's not always about making sure people follow basic laws against sexual harassment. Work culture has become much more collaborative in recent years, and CEOs and managers are realizing that it's easier to get people to work together—and be productive—when they can empathize with one another. Digital consultancy DDI found that, as of 2016, about 20 percent of US employers offered some kind of empathy training for managers. Leaders rated as having high empathy by direct reports are 2.5 times more likely to set clear performance expectations, hold others accountable for maintaining high performance, and address performance issues in a fair and consistent manner, according to data from a DDI meta-analysis. The analysis also found that among more than two thousand direct reports, the number of leaders said to frequently display empathetic behaviors six months after an empathy program rose by 25 percent.

As in the education and journalism industries, empathy is touted as the latest must-have skill to set yourself apart from other job candidates, including those who have a hard-to-beat killer skill of their own: artificial intelligence. Some estimates suggest AI (machines imitating human behavior) could take eight hundred million jobs by 2030, but one thing those bots don't have (at least, not yet) is *emotional* intelligence.

Still, for all that business and technology executives talk about the importance of empathy, they don't often have a prescription for improving it.

Uncovering Unconscious Bias

By her own admission, Natalie Egan spent years living in a bubble. As a successful entrepreneur with highly coveted venture-capital suitors, her experience was far from the norm. At the time, Egan, a transgender woman, looked to the world like a man in an industry dominated by men.

"We're naturally wired with empathy, but I think the particular dynamic I was in can really isolate people from reality and the rest of the world," she told me when we spoke on the phone.

Then she came out as a trans woman, and the empathy gap became clearer to her than it had ever been. As she started to move through the world perceived as a woman instead of as a man, she couldn't help but notice how differently people treated her.

"I went from being in a privileged space to being on the outer edges of one of the most marginalized communities in the world," Egan said.

In a sense, Egan had always known what it was like to be an outlier, but now she would be fully living her life that way. The differences made themselves apparent almost immediately. She suddenly noticed things about her peers in the startup space that she hadn't noticed before—for example, the way they talked about people outside their circle. Egan was still in that circle, but she could now see it differently: Egan herself was subject to offensive language and jokes made at her expense. She remembers experiences while shopping or attempting to conduct a business meeting when people wouldn't look her in the eye.

This is a familiar situation to countless LGBTQ people around the country. And it hurt. But Egan still had the advantage of her education, experience, and network. So she decided to approach the issue of this apparent empathy gap with a startup, and Translator was born. At first, it was meant to be a social network for the transgender community, but pretty soon the mission expanded by necessity. As Egan shopped the idea to investors, she kept running into roadblocks: so many people simply didn't understand the problem she was trying to fix. So, ever flexible and adaptive, Egan reframed again: Translator would take on the job of making the empathy gap clearer, and then try to close it.

She wanted her peers in the business world to understand just how divergent from each other the experiences of people of different genders in the industry could be. Translator soon morphed into a vehicle for technology-assisted diversity-and-inclusion experiences for organizations and corporations of all sizes. The company uses chatbots, apps, and customized virtual-reality experiences to expose employees at organizations like the New York City Department of Education and the consulting giant McKinsey & Company to the experiences of women, gender-nonconforming people, people with disabilities, and people of color around and among them.

When we spoke on the phone, Egan asked me to imagine sitting in a typical diversity-and-inclusion training. I wanted to yawn just thinking about it. In my experience, this usually means sitting in an uncomfortable chair for an uncomfortably long time listening to a long list of uncomfortable scenarios—some of which I have experienced myself, and some I never will: being touched inappropriately, being referred to with a slur, being constantly interrupted by male colleagues, etc. To make things more interesting—and, hopefully, effective—Translator concentrates on a force at the root of most of this behavior: unconscious bias, or the tendency for all of us to internalize and often perpetuate stereotypes about those who are different from us. We might not have conscious thoughts of bias, sexism, racism, or stereotyping, but the culture we live in sometimes makes those things inevitable on an unconscious level. Activists and entrepreneurs like Egan hope to make those unconscious biases more obvious, ideally making them easier to quash.

Translator approaches this in a few different ways, but Egan says the most effective are those that incorporate technology into interactive group activities. One activity commonly used in diversity-and-inclusion workshops is "the privilege walk." Participants line up and take steps forward or backward based on how they identify with statements read by a facilitator. I would take steps forward for "One of my parents works a white-collar job" and "I was told that I was smart and capable by my parents," and steps back for "I've been paid less or treated less fairly because of race, ethnicity, gender, or sexual identity," for example.

I wouldn't move at all for "I was raised in a single-parent household" or "I went to school speaking a language other than English" because those don't apply to me. At the end of the exercise, the different struggles and advantages of everyone in the room become stark based on where they stand. It can be powerful, but it can also be very upsetting—potentially unproductively so—for people who aren't prepared to really understand the context and implications of the exercise. Feeling anxious, embarrassed, and guilty can make empathy pretty difficult.

Translator offers a privilege-walk exercise, but it's conducted anonymously, via smartphone. The results are shared with the whole group, but names are erased. In another module, a Translator facilitator asks people to list all the stereotypes they feel others associate with them, or that they might associate with themselves. A common answer, especially from men and participants of color, Egan told me, is "threat." Instead of doing this on paper, Translator does it through an anonymous web-based app. Suddenly what was once an awkward exercise of reading vulnerable lists in front of coworkers becomes more private, and therefore sometimes more honest. It also has the counterintuitive effect of requiring participation while preserving privacy. Everyone's answers are displayed to the group on a host screen, the anonymized data showing how many people listed each stereotype.

"The group has the experience of learning without having anyone in particular volunteer information," said Egan. Critics argue that this strategy removes responsibility from the exercise, but Egan thinks it actually benefits the most stereotyped people in the room by not "otherizing" them in discussions about marginalization.

In one session with two hundred participants, in less than four minutes the app had captured more than 1,200 stereotypes. The screen at the front of the room showed a huge word cloud of all the words. It was alarming. It looked like about 25 percent of the people in the room believed they were stereotyped as "weak." One woman raised her hand. She looked to be on the verge of crying.

"I thought I knew everyone here," she said. "I had no idea how differently we all see ourselves."

"It was such an interesting statement," Egan said. "She's in a room with two hundred people she had been working with for years. That moment where she realized she may look around and say, 'We all have privilege but we're all kind of the same people,' all of a sudden that got completely blown apart. She was exposed to so many different perspectives of how we see ourselves in the world. That, for her, was a really powerful moment."

Egan admits these exercises sometimes make people angry. "People realize their privilege, but then they're also in a very awkward position in the room with a lot of people who may not have the same level of privilege," she explained. "We had one individual really express in a training how angry they were, not with anyone else, but with themselves. They said, 'Well, what do I do with my privilege?' He had this epiphany moment in front of everybody."

Now Translator is working on an even more visceral experience. The company is building bespoke VR experiences for its clients, some of whom include NBCUniversal, Slack, and Salesforce. Egan described a potential VR experience that will put employees in a work-related situation, a social situation, and on a dark street at night, and help them understand their own biases about different types of people they might come across in each. Rather than simply asking yes-or-no questions, the experience will have the user swipe their hand left or right, engaging them on multiple planes. The feelings that come up in tests of this experience are not always pleasant or charitable, but that's the point. And Egan told me that for people open to the experience, it can have a transformative effect.

"It's amazing, when you change the context, how much people's attitude and behavior shifts," she said.

In describing this phenomenon, Egan evoked what she sees as the three pillars of empathy: self-awareness, peer awareness, and action taking.

"Those three things are hard to bring together in a single training or a single experience, but VR can really help you do that," she said. Self-awareness is immediately impacted by the fact that, during a VR experience, you don't feel like you are yourself. That activates a type of thinking that's hard to simulate just by imagining someone else's experience. "Layer on the idea of identities in context, and you now understand your identity a little better, and it lets you understand the identities of others around you as you interact with them."

This layering also allows Translator to collect a larger amount of data that helps clients see if the experiences are actually making a difference. Egan acknowledges that Translator can't eradicate unconscious bias in an organization, but it can make people more aware of it and at least start conversations about empathy. This is where the communication aspect of empathy comes up once again.

More than Words

If you've ever worked in a startup office, you'll be familiar with a particular kind of quiet—one punctuated only by tap-tapping from keyboards and the occasional sneeze or chair scrape. Everyone sits with earbuds in, listening to music or podcasts or sometimes nothing at all. Most conversations happen via chat programs like Google Hangouts, Skype for Business, and Slack. Even in more traditional offices, it's become common to email someone sitting just a few feet away.

Over email or chat, it's easier to say no to a request without asking questions or really understanding the context, for example. It's hard to grasp tone via text, and many workers report harboring worry, guilt, and frustration with colleagues and bosses based on unclear communications. Employees can also feel less comfortable going to a supervisor with a concern if their relationship is solely web based. (My boss sat in the office next to mine at my old job, but we almost exclusively communicated via chat and email, and I'm certain that contributed, at least in part, to my hesitation in reporting my coworker's inappropriate behavior to her. I felt like I would be "bothering" her if I made a complaint in person, but putting it in writing felt too weighty.)

I spoke to one lawyer and entrepreneur in his early forties who believes the younger generation in the workplace does not have the requisite skills to engage in diverse environments, because they are so used to being "shut off" behind screens, even when collaborating with coworkers. He points to Uber as perhaps the biggest example of how this problem can spread from the individual to the cultural within a corporation. The ride-sharing company reportedly had a deep-seated culture of harassment and intimidation, which drove out a number of female engineers. It seemed to be something of an open secret among some employees—much like the "whisper network" about abusive men in Hollywood that led to the #MeToo movement. It wasn't until former engineer Susan Fowler wrote a scathing essay in early 2017 exposing the problem that many people really thought to question the way Uber, the darling of the sharing economy, operated on the inside. After Fowler's exposé, in which she claimed that Uber's human-resources team ignored her complaints about sexual harassment, the company underwent mass firings, and founder and CEO Travis Kalanick resigned under the pressure of sexual-assault allegations. Fowler wasn't alone, and the projection was that the company's culture had doubly harmed her and her colleagues: first by subjecting them to harassment and unfair treatment, and then by making them feel they couldn't even talk about it. A similar story played out at Google, where employees staged walkouts to protest the internal handling of sexual-harassment claims and signed letters urging the company to drop its Chinese search engine, Project Dragonfly, over concerns about censorship.

"Communication is a lot more than the words you say," the entrepreneur told me.

Adam Waytz, a psychologist and associate professor of management and organizations at Northwestern University's Kellogg School of Management, is skeptical that technology—even VR—can really help with these foundational issues. He isn't sure most companies doing empathy work are on the same page about what empathy means. He acknowledges the effectiveness of empathy training in workplaces but says that is cultivating empathy for a very specific purpose—to improve collaboration and, ultimately, financial returns.

"We do know that empathy matters," Waytz told me. "People who feel that their leaders and managers are empathetic and altruistic feel more free to innovate. They have better teamwork and work harder and make more money."

But what about empathy for its own sake? Perspective-taking is about a lot more than the bottom line.

Waytz thinks corporations have become too obsessed with engagement and getting employees to connect more with customers and coworkers, and aren't letting them do what might actually foster even more empathy: just live.

"There are two ways to improve the dehumanizing crush of the workplace currently," he hypothesized. "Make people feel happier about their work through developing a sense of empathy with coworkers, bosses, teammates, and customers, or just detaching them. I think that would be the most empathetic thing companies could do—just let them go. Empathy is good for engaging people at work, but maybe we should be *disengaging* people from their work."

Waytz doesn't mean laying people off—he means letting people leave early to go have a drink, or hang out with their kids, or play in a band. At the risk of being cheesy, he wants companies to let people work to live, as opposed to the other way around. He points to one thing many of the consistently rated "most empathetic" companies have in common: they have a ton of amenities that ultimately send the message to employees that they should never leave the office.

But even Waytz is intrigued by the potential of empathetic technology in the workplace. He just wants to see proof that it works.

So far, the data on this is minimal, but it seems promising. Paradigm, a strategy firm that does high- and low-tech empathy training, found that 96 percent of participants left their trainings with the intent of engaging in behaviors to reduce bias. And up to eight months after the Paradigm trainings, employees reported a 25 percent increase in the use of more empathetic methods. Paradigm founder and CEO Joelle Emerson, writing in the *Harvard Business Review* in 2017, said that other employees reported they "stopped giving résumés in advance of tech interviews to reduce bias in expectations of a candidate's potential ability." Another employee wrote that, since the training, anytime they witness someone being interrupted, they "speak up to ensure that person can voice their input after the person who interrupted them is done speaking." Google has reported similar findings with its own internal bias trainings.

One major benefit of empathy training for employees that doesn't show up in meta-analyses—yet—is its potential to strengthen one of the few weapons that humans still have over automation in the workplace.

Management consulting giant McKinsey estimates that four to eight hundred million of today's jobs will become automated by 2030. This trend has caused a significant amount of anxiety for blue-collar workers in particular, but other research suggests they shouldn't give up hope to the robots quite yet. A 2015 *Harvard Business Review* study noted that since the 1980s, the occupations with the highest levels of job and wage growth are those that require the most social proficiency. Empathy may not always be explicitly listed as a requirement in these job descriptions, but it's certainly one of the social skills that set human workers apart from automatons.

Hyatt Hotels CEO Mark Hoplamazian is among those looking to capitalize on his industry's humanness. "The practice of empathy is critical to our business," he said at *Fortune*'s Global Forum conference in Guangzhou, China, in 2017. He said Hyatt uses big data and AI, including real-time chatbots, to understand customers better, but that it still needs employees to show empathy when things go wrong. In hiring new workers, the company uses a neuroscience game developed by a firm called Pymetrics to find people with the right soft skills. "We are increasingly looking for ways to decipher how people are wired, especially for hiring purposes," he said.

Fidelity Investments has made a lot of headlines for implementing empathy-building training programs for customer-facing employees. In 2017, the company's emerging technology group, Fidelity Labs, which was looking at how to automate various kinds of tasks, decided to see if virtual reality could help enhance its most valuable human asset: customer service.

"A lot of our customers are going through difficult times—they are dealing with soaring medical costs or the death of a spouse," Adam Schouela, vice president of product management at Fidelity Labs, told me. "At the same time, though, a large proportion of our call-center associates are relatively younger in age. Their parents aren't even retired, so they don't really have an understanding of what those things are like. We need to really give them a way of empathizing with our customer base."

Fidelity's VR simulation works like this: A new call-center associate puts on a headset, takes a call from a "customer," and is transported to the customer's home in what is effectively a virtual house call. It's a bit of a choose-your-own-adventure situation, so the story changes depending on the decisions the associate makes and the questions they ask. In one scenario, the customer is calling to make a withdrawal from their account. The associate asks questions to understand why and when the customer needs the money. In this case, the customer has mounting medical bills, but if the associate digs a bit further, they find out that the customer really needs the money to be able to pay their mortgage, which is due in three days. Unfortunately, even if Fidelity sends the customer a check, it won't clear in time. After explaining this and hanging up with the customer, the virtual experience continues. The associate listens in on a telephone call between the customer and their daughter, who reiterates the problem, and an emotional conversation ensues.

"Seeing and understanding that, and frankly watching the reactions of people who either didn't process the information correctly or understand what those implications were, you feel a physical reaction," said Schouela. "Associates will actually cringe. That's not something we ever get just watching a video, but when you're practically in that person's dining room and see their crutches against the wall and things like that, you get far more emotionally connected and you really understand what they need, as opposed to them just being another one of hundreds of transactions you have to process that day."

So far, it seems to be working. Schouela couldn't give me specific numbers, but he said Fidelity has measured the success of this project by two metrics: employee satisfaction with training, and customer satisfaction with service. Associates have found the VR empathy training far more engaging than the traditional way of training for customer calls, he said. And more importantly, early numbers show a positive difference in customer-satisfaction scores between those who undergo the training and those who do not.

When we spoke in 2017 this was just a proof of concept, but since then Fidelity Investments has started using VR more regularly to help new associates get acquainted with the kind of stories and problems they might encounter, and make mistakes in a safe environment. Schouela said there's no reason it can't one day be used with customers as well. If future clients consent, associates could use audio and visual technology to virtually "be" in their homes for these conversations. Either way, associates will use what they've learned in the empathy-building simulations.

Ultimately, Schouela said that "nothing beats actual real interactions with people in their space." Again, technology isn't a replacement for human contact but a tool to augment it.

In business, that can help improve the bottom line and avoid bad press. In health care, it has the potential to do a lot more: more good, and potentially, if we aren't careful, more damage.

CHAPTER 6

FOR YOUR HEALTH

The experiences we have with doctors and nurses, the people we trust to care for us, can leave a lasting impact, for better or worse. I still remember being seven or eight years old and visiting a doctor who promised me—literally said the word "promise"—that he would not perform a swab on my sore throat, then proceeded to dive right in there and do it anyway when I unsuspectingly opened my mouth to say "ahhh." This experience is nothing compared to the trauma that some people experience in medical settings.

Sometimes it's because a doctor is impatient, unsympathetic, or biased. Research shows that overweight women and women of color receive some of the worst health care in general, as too many doctors insist that any malady must be related to their weight or believe that nonwhite patients require less pain relief. Other times the trauma seems inevitable, no matter how caring the clinician—as with a painful injury, an invasive surgery, or a complicated birth.

Taking care of human beings is a stressful job, especially with long hours and high-stakes settings. I've felt empathy myself for doctors who had to "deal with" my comparatively minor issues, and I can only imagine how frustrating it is to see the same patients with the same problems over and over, no matter what interventions are tried. As with other high-stress careers, those who work in medicine are highly susceptible to burnout, becoming so overwhelmed (and sometimes physically ill) that they can't do their jobs, or, perhaps worse, that they do them incorrectly. To avoid this, many medical professionals learn to block out the most difficult and traumatizing parts of their work.

"After a while, you don't hear the children crying very much," one pediatrician told me. Another doctor—a family physician—told me he and his colleagues sometimes gossip and joke about their patients behind closed doors during long overnight shifts. "You have to blow off steam," he said.

If the threat of burnout is ever-present, the goal—in addition to doing no harm—becomes maintaining the proper level of compassion when face to face with a patient. In the world of medicine, this can be easier said than done. A 2011 review of existing research on self-reported empathy among medical students and residents found that empathy levels declined during medical school and residency. Even students who described themselves as empathetic and enthusiastic about helping patients at the beginning of medical school often ended up feeling much more jaded and burnt out by the time they finished their residencies. This decline matters because positive patient-physician communication, in which empathy and compassion are clear, has been found to actually positively impact patients' health. Research has shown correlations between doctor-patient empathy and better outcomes in quality of life, depression, anxiety, and even blood pressure and blood glucose levels. The authors of the 2011 review, which included eighteen studies published between 1990 and 2010, analyzed the reasons that students and residents felt their own empathy recede over the years. Each study they reviewed measured things slightly differently, so there was no clear answer, but here were some suggestions: increased distress (burnout, reduced quality of life, depression) in med school; mistreatment by superiors or mentors; clinical reality (it's not all about saving lives, unfortunately); social-support problems; inadequate role models;

and in one case, that "the possibility of belonging to an elite and privileged group may induce a rational distancing from the patient."

One of the studies analyzed in the review, published in 2009, was titled "The Devil Is in the Third Year." It surveyed 456 students at Jefferson Medical College (now called Sidney Kimmel Medical College) in New Jersey, five different times—when they entered medical school for the first time and when they left each year. The results showed that empathy scores didn't change much during the first two years, but at the end of the third year, they declined significantly, and empathy remained at that low level through graduation. In the abstract, the authors pointed out the irony that "the erosion of empathy occurs during a time when the curriculum is shifting toward patient-care activities; this is when empathy is most essential."

And yet, many patients find it lacking. One recent George Washington University analysis of audio-recorded meetings between doctors and the families of their young patients found that the doctors "missed the opportunity" to address the families' emotions 26 percent of the time. This wasn't just unkind—those who felt their emotions were not understood also received less information. In 2018, researchers from a handful of European universities came together for an observational study of 945 patients and 51 radiologists, surgeons, and clinical physicians. They had the doctors complete surveys about their own levels of empathy, and patients graded them separately. The results did not match up.

I wasn't surprised when I learned this. I'd experienced the disconnect myself more than my fair share of times.

Improving Doctors' Empathy

On a humid day in the summer of 2014, I was running over the Brooklyn Bridge, just a couple of miles from finishing a sixteen-mile training run for the New York City Marathon. I'd just crested the top of the bridge, tourists walking and biking all around me, when I felt a thump in my chest that stopped me in my tracks.

I took a few deep breaths and my heart seemed to be beating in its normal rhythm again. I was close to finishing the longest run of my life, so I brushed it off and kept going. I made it home, cooled off, and started to lower myself into a bath to help with the muscle aches that were already beginning.

Another thump.

This continued into the night and throughout the next day. I got more and more anxious. At one point, sitting at work, I felt a thump-thump, one right after the other, and decided I needed to go to the emergency room. When I got there I was taken back immediately, and I lay there by myself on the worn sheets, wondering what was happening with my heart, worst-case scenarios flashing through my mind.

A few different nurses came to check on me before I saw a doctor, but I remember only one. He was wearing blue scrubs and had a stethoscope around his neck. He sat spread legged on a stool at the foot of my bed and asked me to describe what I'd been feeling. When I did, he narrowed his eyes.

"Have you felt multiple palpitations in a row?"

Before I could answer, his eyes widened and he added, "Because you know that's not normal, right?"

My chest felt tight and I felt the heart in question speed up. My neck and face flushed.

"I mean . . . I think so, but I can't really be sure?"

He shook his head and stood up. "One palpitation at a time is OK, but it's really not good if there's multiple. That's not normal."

With that, he wrote something down on a clipboard, then got up and walked away. I shifted into full panic-attack mode. Over the next couple of hours, as I waited to speak to a doctor, I heard this nurse joking and laughing with his coworkers, saw him tossing paper into trash cans like mini basketballs, while I lay there petrified, trying to breathe deeply and focus on the rhythmic beeping all around me, almost as if others' normally beating hearts might help mine remember what it was supposed to do.

Finally, a doctor arrived and calmed my fears. After she explained that my heart was healthy, and my palpitations were likely due to stress, she confided that she suffered from the same thing. I would be OK, she said. She smiled and, before discharging me, said that we should both try to relax more.

Years later, with a clean bill of heart health and my stress and anxiety under control, I still think about the nurse who gave me erroneous information that *amplified* my fears, and the doctor who connected with me on a human level.

Teaching doctors to be more empathetic is not a new idea. In fact, there have long been simulation centers and paid actors for just this purpose. In *The Empathy Exams*, essayist Leslie Jamison writes poignantly about medical empathy, with which she has had more experience than most. The book starts with her experience as a medical actor, "playing sick" for medical students in simulated exam-room environments. These simulations end with checklists for each actor to fill out based on the medical student's performance. Item 31, Jamison writes, is: "voiced empathy for my situation/problem." But the student's actual empathy for her is measured in many other ways. After doing this so many times—and having so many real medical experiences—she starts to sense the script. "That must really be hard," every doctor seems to say about everything. Jamison writes:

> Empathy isn't just remembering to say *that must really be hard*—it's figuring out how to bring difficulty into the light so it can be seen at all. Empathy isn't just listening, it's asking the questions whose answers need to be listened to. Empathy requires inquiry as much as imagination.

Empathy requires knowing you know nothing. Empathy means acknowledging a horizon of context that extends perpetually beyond what you can see.

That's a lot to ask of a doctor or surgeon, let alone a medical student. Frankly, it's a lot to ask of most people, but we do. Among the things we expect from those we trust to take care of us, empathy is high on the list, even if we don't think about it quite so explicitly. But as Jamison poignantly points out in *The Empathy Exams*, empathy is often not enough for the patient. When Jamison was seeing a doctor for a dangerous and tricky problem with her own heart, she appreciated his calmness and assurance, which she notes might have been evidence of empathy but didn't quite have the effect of an explicit empathic effort. "I needed to look at him and see the opposite of my fear," she writes, "not its echo."

From the provider's perspective, a focus on empathy—explicit or not—can cause an echo in the other direction, leading to anxiety, stress, and ultimately burnout. And to many, introducing a tech-focused fix seems like just another task on an ever-lengthening to-do list.

Many doctors would balk at the idea of adding more technology to their already hardware- and software-burdened jobs. The advent of the electronic health record, which was meant to make updating and sharing health information seamless, has caused a great deal of additional stress and burnout. But research has shown that the introduction of intentional, targeted technology can improve physician empathy and, along with it, patients' experiences and outcomes. In one 2011 study, a group of oncologists were given audio lessons in how to be more empathetic toward their patients with cancer, and CD-ROMs with specific feedback on their own recorded conversations with patients. A control group did not get the additional CD-ROM material. The results: those who had access to the extra information on the CD-ROMs were perceived as more empathetic by patients, who trusted them more.

Now, instead of CD-ROMs, we have apps, algorithms, and virtual reality. In an already slow-to-change industry (that has the added worry of being responsible for, you know, human life) it can be hard to implement a new email system, let alone any of this other, newer technology. But in my search for people using tech to address the empathy problem in medicine, I came across a few who have managed to make the benefits clear enough that they're convincing doctors and hospitals to sign on, and they're getting results.

The Power of Simulation

Medical schools and professionals have gotten used to live, room-scale simulations like the ones described by Leslie Jamison in *The Empathy Exams*. They understand the mandate to act as if a manikin is a real person undergoing cardiac arrest or in need of an appendectomy. Medical simulation has been in use by schools and hospitals since at least the 1930s. One of the most important benefits of it has been that surgeons can practice without having to cut an actual person open. There are large technology centers at medical schools and hospitals around the world dedicated to this purpose. Emerging technologies also allow medical students to see things from their colleagues' perspectives: an anesthesiologist can see what a nurse sees, for example, ostensibly facilitating better teamwork through empathy. Students and professionals used to have to fly out to dedicated centers for this kind of training. Now there are dozens of medical-simulation products available to medical providers and educators, and many use VR. The market is forecast to reach $2.5 billion over the next few years.

It's a comforting thought—that when your doctor or surgeon comes at you with an instrument, or bad news, they've likely practiced many times on actors and inanimate objects. And there's a lot of evidence to suggest that this kind of training works. But practicing conversations with patients can only go so far in terms of the provider's empathy. So health-care students and professionals have started experimenting with what it's like to be on the other side. Most people—doctors included—have been patients at some point in their lives, but not everyone has encountered every condition (thankfully) and most medical professionals will only have the perspective of their own specialty. There's a growing number of medical-technology companies working to close those gaps. They call what they do "tele-empathy."

In some cases, the tech is fairly simple. In 2017, a researcher from the University of Huddersfield in the UK found that wearing temporary tattoos that looked like melanomas helped doctors better understand how their affected patients were feeling. The biggest impact was the emotional toll of having a visible reminder of the cancer, an element not present in many other such diseases.

In Toronto, the technologists at Klick Labs have taken "feel my pain" to the next level with the creation of SymPulse, a device that allows providers to literally feel tremors like those felt by patients with Parkinson's disease and other disorders that affect movement. The idea is that unlike a typical immersive experience, SymPulse delivers a literal jolt of empathy—the doctor doesn't have to imagine how difficult it is to button a shirt or open a door with a painful and shaking hand, they can feel it.

You can watch YouTube videos of people testing out the device. It does not look fun. People grimace, even cry. In one video created by Klick Labs, identical twins test out the SymPulse. One has Parkinson's, the other does not. They both wear contraptions on their arms, and the affected brother is able to essentially transfer his tremors to his twin. It's a moving experience for both of them—the brother with Parkinson's feels understood in a new way, and his twin has a better understanding of how difficult simple things, like giving a thumbs-up, can be with this disease.

Klick calls the concept "symptom transference" and has said it hopes to do the same with diabetes and chronic obstructive pulmonary disease. In addition to empathy, the technology has practical applications—a doctor miles away from a patient could receive real-time symptom information transmitted from the patient's body to an app, helping with a more accurate diagnosis; assessment of improvement after an injury could be more precise with a SymPulse; and providers could make better recommendations for home care for the elderly once they have a clearer sense of an individual elderly patient's physical abilities.

Klick isn't the only one working on symptom-transference devices. Amy Cowperthwait, a nurse in Delaware, noticed an empathy gap during her nearly three decades working in an emergency room. So in 2015 she founded Avkin, which makes wearable technology with haptic feedback (physical sensations for the user, like vibrations or pulses), to be used in education and training settings. Actors wear Avkin's Avtrach (tracheostomy simulation), Avstick (blood-draw simulation), or Avcath (catheter-placement simulation) devices, all of which are anatomically correct and come in three different skin tones and can feel and respond to vibrations and pressure. The devices themselves can also emit sounds and even smells.

The SymPulse and Avkin products could be revolutionary improvements in both empathy and physical care, but right now SymPulse is still a proof of concept, and Avkin is still in startup mode. While the companies work to quantify the impacts of their devices and bring in investments to take them to scale, medical students and professionals can access similar simulation experiences through VR.

The Power and Pitfalls of Embodiment

During Carrie Shaw's freshman year of college, when she was nineteen, the symptoms that had been plaguing her mother for years were diagnosed as early-onset Alzheimer's. It was a difficult time that lasted for the next twelve years. Shaw struggled to balance the process of figuring out her own life with taking on a caregiver role for her mother.

Shaw, who had studied public health at the University of North Carolina at Chapel Hill, crisscrossed the country in search of an anchor. She spent some time in Seattle hoping to find work at a nonprofit, then went to the Dominican Republic with the Peace Corps. Her experience was similar to that of many Peace Corps participants: "My job was to be a health educator and I showed up there and realized, as idealistic and helpful as I hoped to be, I just really didn't get the culture, I didn't know the language, and having to teach reproductive health given those things . . . it was at first pretty mysterious."

She tried to combat the mystery with art, which she had turned to during other times of confusion. "I found that was about the only useful thing I could provide," she told me over the phone from LA, where she runs Embodied Labs, a company that makes VR patient simulations for health-care students and workers. "I found that if I could draw what I was teaching and tell a good story, it could really transcend culture, language, and even education barriers."

This realization would eventually lead to a master's degree in medical illustration. But it was an experience she had while again living with her parents and helping to develop her mother's home health-care plan that sparked the idea for Embodied Labs.

Shaw's mother's condition had led to a deficit in her left field of vision—she couldn't see out of the left halves of both of her eyes. This turned out to be frustratingly difficult to explain to home health aides. Even with a drawing, it was still hard for some of them to remember that Shaw's mother needed to always be approached from the right side and that her left side needed extra protection. So Shaw decided to demonstrate in a different way. She taped off the left half of each lens in a pair of goggles and had each aide try them on.

"It was like, 'Here's her perspective,' and we could intuitively all feel why you'd have to rotate her food for her," Shaw said.

This simple solution to a complex home-health-care issue got her thinking: Why was it so hard to understand what people with brain diseases were going through? And if we could do that better, how might care be transformed?

Rita Addison, a psychotherapist-turned-photographer, might have been the first to use virtual reality to get people to see and feel a medical condition from the perspective of a sufferer. In 1994, Addison released *Detour: Brain Deconstruction Area Ahead*, a disorienting and haunting virtual-reality experience meant to simulate the way she experienced the world after suffering a traumatic brain injury. The work—pixelated and simple by today's standards, but technically impressive for 1994— begins with a stylized reenactment of the car accident that caused her injury, complete with screeching tires and Addison's own moans. The bulk of the experience takes place in a simulated art gallery. Addison's nature photography is displayed on the walls, but both the photographs and the walls refuse to maintain one shape or texture. There are constant frightening sounds in the background as the viewer tries to focus on the art despite an ever-changing visual field; a black circle occasionally takes up much of the frame, and the lights and colors seem to change on a whim. It's not a pleasant experience, which was, of course, the point. As Addison told virtual-reality performer and blogger Galen Brandt, she had hoped a VR experience could make the invisible—the confusing and painful world she inhabited as she recovered—visible to others. "Maybe I could create a therapeutic environment that immersed them in an 'undivided moment' of deepened, altered awareness so that they could transcend their own consciousness and experience the psychic relief of total empathy with another's experience," she said.

Addison's feelings of discombobulation certainly came through when I watched a video of this experience, but the 1990s quality didn't quite lead me to transcendence. Considering how far the technology has come, I almost worry that a current iteration of *Detour* might trigger a panic attack for me.

Embodied Labs' first simulation started as a wonky animated experience too. Shaw quickly discovered what they needed was a more human element. She called on an artist friend to help create a workflow that would integrate live-action film and Leap Motion—a technology that uses hand sensors to read finger motions as input, somewhat like a computer mouse—as well as computer-generated stories to make a first-person embodied experience. They wrote the script with help from interviews with dozens of people with macular degeneration and hearing loss and their doctors and caretakers. What they ended up with was a massive file that came to be affectionately known as Alfred, and eventually became a simulation called the Alfred Lab.

Steeped in interviews and research from the tech world, I asked Shaw what ALFRED was an acronym for.

"Well, the point was to say you're embodying a person," Shaw said patiently. "I don't know if it was a very whimsical decision on my part."

The simulated people that medical students, providers, and home caregivers can embody using Embodied Labs software don't have names like Siri or Cortana—they're Alfred, Beatriz, Clay, and Dima. But these experiences aren't really about whimsy—they're about stepping into the shoes of someone dealing with a degenerative disease. And part of the point is for them to be more relatable than robots.

A group of medical students and educators at the University of Illinois were the first to become Alfred. Shaw recounted for me what it was like to watch them. As Alfred, they would start in a birthday scene, feeling excited about the party happening all around them in virtual reality. Then there's a scene in which Alfred starts to daydream, and the user experiences walking up to a mountaintop, playing with interactive flowers, and listening to beautiful music.

"He's, like, spacing out, basically," she said. "In that scene he has no vision or hearing impairment, and people would laugh out loud and just be really playful in that scene. And then it throws you back into Alfred's story."

Alfred knocks over a glass while daydreaming, and the people around him react in ways that tend to annoy and offend those wearing the VR headset. They report feeling isolated and frustrated when an actor portraying Alfred's son says to a nearby nurse, "You know, he's hard of hearing, so we try to talk loudly to him." People trying the simulation felt like they were being talked down to.

The process of creating this scene was a lesson in empathy for Shaw herself. She and her team had told the actors to treat the camera like it was their grandfather.

"People started saying, 'All they're doing is talking to me like I'm a child.' Then I had this moment where I was talking to my own grandfather, who is pretty much a lip reader, and I was listening to myself and thinking . . . 'Oh, I sound kind of condescending right now!'"

In the months since, the team at Embodied Labs have worked out the kinks and have built a user experience that they hope delivers on a system called "prepare, embody, reflect." It's a way to measure learning and output so medical educators and providers can see what people are actually getting out of these experiences. At the end of each VR module, users are asked to quantify how much knowledge they gained and what specific care practices they learned about. Embodied Labs can track how that knowledge grows over time.

It's not easy to get this kind of technology into the elder-care space. The industry is relatively conservative and is not known as a hotbed of tech innovation; in her research, Shaw noticed that many elder-care facilities and senior homes don't even have Wi-Fi. But she told me that more than forty initial customers in the elder-care industry are using the software, and as of fall 2018 Embodied Labs had about $250,000 in revenue. This is surely thanks in part to the way the company is able to quantify its impact, but it's also a sign of the times: the population of people over the age of sixty-five is growing rapidly in the US. Sometimes called the "age wave" or the "silver tsunami," this demographic shift is increasing the need for innovation in elder care.

Empathy-building VR could be a great way to help caregivers—professional and otherwise—understand what their elderly patients and family members need. But there's another way VR is being used in the medical field, among patients of all ages, that has Shaw and others a little concerned. When it's done right, it can be hugely positive, but when it's simply "sending old people to the beach in VR," or "pretending to be disabled for six minutes," it can feel more exploitative than anything else.

As Emily Ladau, the writer and disability-rights activist, reminded me: especially in the medical field, technology can only be a supplement, never a replacement for reality.

Ladau recounted an experience from college, in which someone wanted to borrow one of her wheelchairs for a disability event. "You want to take my very expensive piece of equipment I had to fight with my insurance to get covered so people can play around with it in an obstacle course and supposedly understand what my life is like?" she asked, incredulous. "Absolutely not."

Ladau believes technology like VR provides an opportunity to simulate an experience like this without harming or inconveniencing the people you're trying to understand, but she encourages those who use this kind of tool to do it in context—preferably a context that includes real people with disabilities.

"I think we have to remember that technology is amazing, but there are still limitations you're not going to be able to overcome without human interaction," she said. "Even in a hospital or a medical-school setting, the best thing you can do is talk to people."

But VR isn't only for the nondisabled hoping to better understand others' experiences. It's increasingly being used as a simulation for patients themselves.

Getting Distracted

In the summer of 2017 I came across a study that showed that "visiting" a beach via Oculus Rift VR headset while undergoing dental work was such an effective distraction that it reduced patients' anxiety and even gave them more positive memories of the experience. Yes, positive memories of a visit to the dentist. In the study, which I wrote about for VICE News's health section, Tonic, researchers from the Universities of Plymouth, Exeter, and Birmingham in England teamed up with a dental practice to test the effects of animated VR experiences. One allowed patients to hang out at a local beach, and another let them walk through a virtual city. The beach scene was really nice to look at, even in regular 2-D video—it was an English bay, so instead of bright hot sun and umbrellas, the video showed hills covered in both sand and grass, grazing horses, and gently lapping waves against an orange sunset. The study included a control group who just had a regular dental visit. Afterward, the researchers found that those who visited the virtual beach were less anxious and happier with their experience than either of the other two groups.

It's not uncommon to be instructed by a doctor or nurse to "think of your favorite place" during a blood-pressure reading or to squeeze a partner's hand during labor pains. Sometimes the idea is to distract and calm you; sometimes it's just so you can *feel* like you're distracting and calming yourself in the hope that the placebo effect might work in your favor. Increasingly, VR is being used to make distraction from unpleasant medical situations more immersive.

In Australia, pediatrician Evelyn Chan spent a lot of time, as she put it, "popping lots of needles into kids." This language might sound harsh, but Chan is anything but. She's a slight woman with long dark hair, impeccable posture, and a soft voice. She essentially has the demeanor of the prototypical pediatrician. When we met in the summer of 2018, we sat perpendicular to each other at a big white table. As she described the needle sticks and blood draws she had to do for children, she visibly winced.

"It's incredibly stressful for the child and, in turn, for families. It's the most feared part of the experience in hospital, and it's very common, so they dread it daily," she told me. As a pediatrician, she admitted that she eventually developed a thick skin. "I always found it really hard and wondered what we could do, something between simple toys and distraction and having to restrain or give anesthetic."

She thought VR seemed like an interesting idea but wasn't sure how it would translate to the hospital setting. Then a colleague told her that his grandmother, who had dementia, had been ecstatic after walking through her old hometown in Italy via a VR headset. She had started speaking Italian again and remembering things from photos and videos that she hadn't remembered in years. Chan thought that if VR could do that, maybe it could help sick kids too.

The concept Chan came up with is called Smileyscope. In a clinical trial published in the *Journal of Pediatrics* in 2019, she and her coauthors found that 252 children aged four to eleven who used Smileyscope in emergency rooms and outpatient labs experienced a 60 percent decrease in needle pain, 75 percent decrease in distress, and 50 percent decrease in the need for restraints. Smileyscope is now being used in hospitals in the United States and Australia, where kids who use the headset experience an underwater animation complete with fish and dolphins as a voiceover explains their procedure.

I was skeptical about how magical this transformation seemed until I watched a video of a young burn victim during a presentation by Walter Greenleaf, an expert in VR and AR in medicine at Stanford University.

He pulled up a video of a young boy wearing a VR headset in a hospital bed. The boy had bandages on his arm—Greenleaf explained that he'd survived an awful-sounding event called "degloving" in which the skin on his arm had essentially been peeled off by a burn. Needless to say, changing the bandages was excruciating. He began to dread seeing nurses and doctors come into his room, and he would thrash and cry; the anticipation started to become almost as miserable as the task itself. Until someone put a headset on him. We all watched as the child in the video moved his head around, smiling, as someone attended to his wounded arm. By pairing these VR sessions, in which the child got to explore an underwater world, with painful routine care, a new association was created in his mind. He was still in pain, no doubt, but he began almost to look forward to these sessions, and he no longer panicked as they drew near.

There is some empirical evidence to show that this technique works at a larger scale as well. AppliedVR, a company that spun off from a global marketing-research firm, creates experiences to address acute pain and anxiety, discomfort during labor and delivery, and chronic pain, mostly in hospital settings. Vangelis Lympouridis, AppliedVR's chief designer, says the platform is already being used by more than 250 hospitals and more than 30,000 patients. And the company has the data to back itself up: randomized independent research has shown a 52 percent reduction in pain levels for 120 patients at Cedars-Sinai and a 31 percent reduction in pain and 24 percent reduction in anxiety in kids at Children's Hospital Los Angeles.

The benefits extend from the patients to their families, and also to the providers themselves. Chan talked about not being able to hear children crying after a while, but the truth was she could still hear it, and the more she blocked it out, the more susceptible to burnout she became. That's why this kind of technology might also be a solution for physicians. It allows a level of tech-assisted empathy to take place without much effort required of the doctor.

"For clinicians it really helps," said Chan, "because it's a tool that helps reframe the experience, the child tends to have a better outcome, and there's also less risk of needle-stick injuries to clinicians themselves."

VR pain distraction isn't for everyone. People with epilepsy, for example, might have their condition triggered by a VR experience. People who are extremely sick probably don't need something strapped to their face; the same is true for people with very high anxiety. This has posed a unique challenge in the growing area of assistive technology for people—especially children—with autism. But Vijay Ravindran thinks he has the solution.

Connecting with Kids with Autism Spectrum Disorder

In fall 2015, tech entrepreneur Vijay Ravindran got the chance to try out the latest version of the Oculus VR headset, and he knew almost immediately that he had to share the experience with his young son, who has ASD (autism spectrum disorder) and a deep fascination with Google Maps. When Ravindran's son put on the headset, he quickly understood how to use it. He figured out how the positional tracking worked, how to flip between different views, and how to navigate Google Maps to his own neighborhood in VR.

"He went to our neighborhood Starbucks, he was cruising around town, just really happy," Ravindran told me over the phone from Maryland. "After he took off the headset, he talked with us in a different way that both my wife and I noticed."

Ravindran, a software engineer by training, and his wife, a computer-science professor, pay close attention to the way their son acts, speaks, and plays because he is autistic, and they are always thinking about the best ways to engage him and help him express himself. Watching him enjoy his time in the Oculus, and seeing how that experience bled into life outside the headset, created the spark of an idea. Ravindran's wife, Vibha Sazawal, was the first to say it out loud: "This could be used for therapy."

Ravindran, who had led software engineering at Amazon and founded several startups, wasn't sure at first that VR was ready for kids—especially kids with autism, who, though their traits and experiences vary, tend to have different sensitivities and learning styles from neurotypical kids. But both Ravindran and Sazawal knew there was something to the impact the Oculus experience had had on their child, and they thought it could scale—not just for entertainment and fun, but for training in the social skills that can be difficult for kids on the autism spectrum. After watching their son and other children use the Oculus, they realized that if they wanted to make a therapeutic or educational impact, they needed a way to see what the child was seeing in the headset. They designed a livestream of the headset view to a second device that could also control the experience, and they launched a software-and-hardware company in 2016 called Floreo.

When we spoke, Ravindran was careful to note that Floreo is not an FDA-approved treatment or therapy for autism. He and his colleagues deliberately refer to it as "social-skills training using VR." The social skills it focuses on are "building-block skills" needed for things like eye contact, raising a hand in the classroom, staying in line, and "joint attention," or paying attention to something—like a television show or a teacher's lesson—at the same time someone else is paying attention to it.

In one Floreo experience, the child hears an animal make a noise, and is asked by the person controlling the experience—a parent or, more often, a teacher—to find that animal. When the child turns his or her head toward the animal, there's a visual reward—an animated burst of stars, in this case.

"The camera view gives an exact sense of what the kids are seeing, and many teachers and therapists say that even if they're in the same room as someone with autism, there's something special in seeing literally what they're seeing, how they're panning across an area, how they gaze on something," Ravindran said. "That perspective is really powerful."

School can be difficult for kids with autism not only because certain social lessons are harder to learn; many also have trouble because of the cacophony of sounds and colors and lights in the school environment. Some schools have installed sensory break rooms where kids can find respite for a while and then rejoin the regular classroom, but Ravindran says these can cost upward of $50,000. He hopes that Floreo, which costs about $50 a month for the app plus the cost of a VR headset (starting at around $200), can serve as a more affordable alternative, a sort of portable, accessible version of a sensory break room.

I had heard of similar tools meant to help kids with autism learn social skills in the safety of VR, but Floreo's experiences can also take things a step further, out of the classroom and into the street in a way that I could see being controversial. The company is developing VR experiences to help prepare young people with autism for more serious situations, like going through a TSA line and boarding an airplane, for example, or engaging with police.

My first reaction when I heard about the police simulation was confusion. *Is this really necessary for a kid?* I wondered. But during a presentation I sat in on, Ravindran explained to the audience how dangerous a police encounter can be for a person with autism and their caregivers.

He reminded the group of a 2016 incident in Florida in which a person with autism wandered from his home. As his caregiver tried to get hold of him, he was acting erratically and someone called the police, who interpreted the situation as dangerous and shot the caregiver. Ravindran said that even years later, when he talked to families with autism, this incident was seared into their memories. It could have happened to any of their kids, they said, and they wanted to be prepared.

Now Floreo is working on NIH-funded research aimed at creating VR experiences to help families navigate similar situations. That research is the basis of a simulated police interaction in which the viewer has the perspective of a child with autism as two police officers approach and begin to ask questions. The user—usually a person with ASD—can choose from several options in response, and an aide working with the user can follow along and assess. The experience includes coaching on how to respond to police questions with key identifying information, such as name and address. In the initial VR lessons the officers are friendly, but they get increasingly less so as the lessons go on. The idea is to make people with autism more comfortable with situations that might be unfamiliar or frightening, and to allow them to practice answering with composure in case their words or actions are misinterpreted as dangerous by police. Ravindran said Floreo gets a lot of requests for experiences that are flipped, in which adults—including police officers—could do VR encounters to learn how to better communicate with people who have ASD.

"The first thing you learn when you start interacting with multiple kids with autism is that autism manifests in so many different ways—the challenges of one are not the challenges of all," Ravindran told me.

That being said, there are some challenges that many kids with autism share—for example, having a hard time knowing whether someone is being friendly or teasing or bullying. Floreo is currently developing a module that takes place in a middle-school hallway. The user encounters a few different characters—some friendly, some not, some neutral. The goal is to be able to tell the difference, which can be hard for any kid. Ravindran said he sees a big opportunity for expanding into modules that teach perspective-taking and understanding others' feelings.

"That's definitely an area we work on at home a lot with my son, and it's not one where there's a lot of training provided to kids," he said. "Our goal is to go where they want to go, where they see challenges."

In that vein, each module is only fifteen minutes long, with two five-minute lessons and a five-minute break in between. Floreo also provides data that isn't as easy to get through conventional therapy, which Ravindran says differentiates it from the many other programs that parents and teachers of kids with autism are often bombarded with. The next step, he hopes, will be modules for adults with autism, helping them find employment and take advantage of their particular strengths.

Bigger names in tech have taken up similar work. Google Glass launched a prototype software to help children with autism learn social skills and practice conversations. In 2017, a study published in the journal *Frontiers in Robotics and AI* found that it worked pretty well—it recognized conversational prompts from the children and responded in a convincing way, so most kids were comfortable enough talking to it that they saw some improvement.

Software that talks back might seem counterintuitive, but as I've learned, AI systems are quickly becoming normal parts of our everyday life, and they increasingly are being given not only intelligence but personality.

Neuroscience and philosophy researchers at the University of Freiburg, in Germany, came together to study the use of socially assistive robots and found that as the population expands and people live longer, the demand for humanlike robot assistance will continue to grow. Some researchers have worried that we already expect too much from these bots: technical flawlessness, personality, adaptation to environments, behavioral changes based on our needs, and, in the medical context as well as others, empathy.

We are relying ever more on technology, from VR to AI, for connection that we once sought from caregivers, family members, and friends. Are we outsourcing empathy? And if so, is that necessarily a bad thing?

CHAPTER 7
BEST BOT FRIENDS

The question of whether a robot could have empathy, or if it even should, was not at the top of my list when I first started thinking about the integration of robots into human life. Instead I imagined whether a robot would someday clean my house or cook a meal without my having to lift a finger to help. I daydreamed about whether the robots I would eventually share my life with might be cute like Rosie, my favorite cartoon robot from *The Jetsons*, or enormous and terrifying like the title character of *The Iron Giant*, or murderous like the androids in *The Terminator*. So when I first started researching human-computer interaction, I didn't expect to find too much information about empathy. I figured the top minds in robotics would be busy trying to make sure robots didn't steal all our jobs or take up arms against us. But reality is, of course, a little less dramatic than sci-fi, even if the line between the two seems to be blurring every day. While effects on unemployment and safety are important to artificial-intelligence developers, empathic AI—and more broadly, human-computer communication—are actually pretty high on the priority list as well. And if you take a quick inventory of the gadgets all around you, it might be obvious why that is.

Many of us already use robots every day without much thought, though they don't look quite how we used to expect them to look. Instead of Rosie the Robot rolling through our midcentury-modern homes in the sky, bringing us drinks and making jokes, we have Siri, Alexa, Google, and Cortana, always listening for our call and trying to assist us with basic tasks. They are much more unassuming physically, but they know everything—at least, everything that Apple, Amazon, Google, and Microsoft know, including our whereabouts and what we like to listen to and buy.

As I wrote this, the red ring of light on top of my Amazon Echo caught my eye from across the room. The light was red because the microphone was off. I had won the device at a conference and been hesitant to even bring it home. I acknowledge the irony of this as someone who writes about the potential positive side of humanlike tech, but products like Alexa make me feel conflicted. I'm not a conspiracy theorist—I don't think the government is using gadgets like Alexa to spy on me and my husband (wow, would their reports be boring if they were). But I know enough to realize that some ideas that sound like conspiracies are actually true—Amazon does indeed have the capability to listen to me and my husband talk (and our cat hiss and yell for dinner, I assume). That's how this device gets to know the people it's meant to help with recommendations. Amazon, Apple, and other major tech companies say that privacy measures are in place, but I've had enough creepy experiences—seeing ads on Instagram for items I just bought in a brick-and-mortar store, for example—to be wary. My husband, on the other hand, loves the idea of being able to ask Alexa for a measurement conversion or to play a certain song. So we compromised. I brought the Echo home, and when my husband is home by himself, he talks to Alexa as much as he wants; when I'm home, her microphone is off.

And yes, when we talk about Alexa, we sometimes use the pronoun *her* without thinking. It's so easy to slip into anthropomorphizing these robots, not least because they have human names. That's part of their appeal. In fact, creators of these personal digital assistants take advantage of this tendency, putting a lot of thought into the names, voices, and even tones. The companies that create them want us to feel like these bots care about us, even if, intellectually, we know they don't. But what if they did?

Ellie, a digital avatar who interviews potential therapy patients, might be a peek into this possible future. Created by researchers at the University of Southern California to assess psychological stress, Ellie puts people at ease not only as well as a human therapist—in some cases, she's gotten better results.

About 30 percent of Vietnam veterans, 12 percent of Gulf War veterans, and 15 percent of veterans of the wars in Iraq and Afghanistan have symptoms of PTSD, that we know of. Many service members and veterans say they avoid seeking help for mental-health concerns because of the stigma. The US Department of Veterans Affairs (VA) can't count—or help—those who don't come forward. Enter Ellie: an unassuming and pleasant piece of AI, represented on a screen by a computer-generated brown-haired woman in a cardigan sitting in a comfortable-looking chair.

Ellie, one of several kinds of therapeutic technologies available to some veterans, has a calm demeanor, as much as a digital avatar can have a demeanor at all. Her face is pleasant, and she smiles without seeming too happy. She asks basic questions about the veteran's or service member's life and whether there's anything they'd like to talk about. Her goal is to track behavior and try to identify signs of psychological distress. She is the "eyes and ears" of a more complex project called SimCoach, an online interactive health-care guide for military veterans and their families, according to project leader Albert "Skip" Rizzo. Ellie might ask whether a person has had bad dreams about their combat experiences, or whether they're bothered by obsessive thoughts—choosing what to ask, and when, based on the veteran's facial expressions, which she monitors by tracking speech patterns and sixty-six different points on their face.

Ellie, unassuming and anonymous, gets results. According to research conducted by Rizzo and others at USC, those who spoke to her were more open about their symptoms than they had been when filling out a required military assessment. The results of those assessments have to be reported, potentially affecting career prospects. To many, speaking out loud to Ellie—an attentive but nonjudgmental piece of technology—felt safer. "It's a humanlike interaction," one of the researchers told CNBC, without the very human worry about exposing oneself to reprimand or stigma. Ellie is able to convey a sense of empathy while maintaining enough distance that people trained to hide their emotions can feel comfortable accessing and expressing them. This allows veterans to get negative feelings and concerns off their chests, while also allowing the technology to track word choice and tone, which can sometimes point to signs of depression or suicidal ideation.

"By receiving anonymous feedback from a virtual human interviewer that they are at risk for PTSD, they could be encouraged to seek help without having their symptoms flagged on their military record," psychologist Gale Lucas, who worked on Ellie, said in a statement when the technology was introduced.

I watched a split-screen demo with a young man on one side and Ellie on the other. She started the conversation by saying, "I'm not a therapist, but I'm here to learn about people and would love to learn about you. I'll ask a few questions to get us started, and please feel free to tell me anything—your answers are totally confidential." I could see the man's face relax a little. He told her where he was from and how he was doing. At the end of the demo, Ellie asked, "When was the last time you felt really happy?" and the man began to open up.

There is one catch, though. Ellie is currently operated by researchers who don't work for the military. If and when she becomes integrated into the military health system, the anonymity might be lost. If a service member needs a mental-health intervention, a real person still has to be the one to do that. Lucas and her team have said they hope to counteract any hesitancy this may cause in veterans by requiring Ellie to alert humans only if a service member threatens to hurt themselves or someone else. Generally Ellie's creators plan to leave it up to the individual whether to follow up their AI session by meeting with a real doctor.

The veterans who speak to Ellie seem to like her both because she *acts like* a human, expressing concern, interest, and empathy, and also because she *is not* a human. If that seems contradictory, it's a good depiction of how unsure many of us still are about how to feel about bots.

We Have a Lot of Feelings about Robots

The ways humans interact with robots can be frustratingly contradictory. Anecdotal research over the past two decades has shown that some people are more prone to feeling emotionally attached to computers than others. One longitudinal field study of six elderly people found that while two of them adapted to the presence of a cute rabbit-shaped robot named Nabaztag as if it were a real animal companion (giving it a new name, talking to it, etc.), the other four either weren't sure how they felt about it or saw it more as a tool. Though new information about human-robot interaction is constantly being gathered, the results still haven't yet led to clear answers.

Human-robot-interaction researchers have even replicated the historic Milgram experiment, in which Yale psychologist Stanley Milgram claimed to show how far people will go to obey authority by asking participants to apply shocks to a screaming person in another room. (Milgram's results—in which 40 percent of participants stopped before reaching maximum voltage—were recently shown to have been manipulated.) In 2006 and 2008, Christoph Bartneck, of the Human Interface Technology Lab in New Zealand, and his colleagues found that all twenty of their research subjects were willing to apply the highest voltage to a robot with facial expressions that could move and talk. On the other hand, while all participants in a later study involving Microbug robots (little crawling toys) complied with instructions to destroy the bots with a hammer, they felt bad about it. Some said they didn't enjoy "killing" the "poor robot" because it was "innocent."

Participants in these surveys—even children, for the most part—understand intellectually that robots and toys cannot really be "innocent" any more than they can be "evil." Just like I know that Alexa is not a real person with feelings. But the more these bots seem to *express* feelings toward us, the more our subconscious seems to recognize them, even at a low level, as fellow humans. Empathy for robots can seem to serve no purpose. Why should it matter to someone how a robot feels if it's turned off? Why should a Microbug be protected from being smashed, when it won't feel anything? Why should I worry about offending or annoying Alexa by turning her off? Oddly, I sometimes do.

A study by Peter Kahn of the University of Washington in 2012 brought it all home for me: 98 percent of children who participated were against putting a person in a closet, and 100 percent said it was OK to put a broom there—but only 54 percent were OK with putting a robot called Robovie in the closet. They knew the robot wasn't a person, but they still felt bad treating it inhumanely. Researchers said the children showed signs of empathy as well as confusion about how to respond to the experience of an inanimate object. I can relate. I know my Amazon Echo is not a person—"Alexa" is not in there, she's just an algorithm with a voice. And yet, when she misunderstands my husband and he swears at her, I feel a little bad. And when I turn her microphone off, I do sometimes have a sense that I'm shutting out some*one*, rather than just something.

Robot makers know we feel things for their creations. A couple of ostensibly lovable bots called Jibo and Kuri have been disappointments, either because people found them unnerving or because their technology wasn't quite up to expectations. But humans still want to keep trying. At the 2019 Consumer Electronics Show, Lovot, a robot designed specifically to be cuddled and taken care of, made lots of headlines.

There is some research that might help explain this phenomenon. In 2018, German researchers published a study in the open-access journal *PLOS ONE* about what happened when eighty-five people were given the choice to switch off a robot they had either just been chatting with or just been using in some functional way. Some of the robots also said out loud that they did not want to be turned off. The results showed that people preferred to keep the bot on when it protested. The participants seemed to be less stressed about turning off the bots that had only been helping them do a task, which wasn't too surprising. But participants had the hardest time turning off robots that both were functional *and* objected to being turned off. The researchers guessed this was because of the emotional dissonance that scenario created in the subjects' minds.

Even at the neurological level, we seem to be unsure of how to handle robots. In 2014, a different group of German researchers had hypothesized that when watching humans and robots being treated nicely or violently, subjects' emotion-processing brain regions would be activated. This turned out to be true. The researchers found that subjects' brain activity upon seeing nicely treated humans and robots was similar, but there was a significant variance between viewing violent human-human interactions and violent human-robot ones: subjects showed more emotion for the humans being harmed. In other studies that measured participants' skin temperature, people seemed to become agitated when the robot was abused.

The story of Pleo, a $500 robotic dinosaur studied in a 2014 experiment, illustrates the problem in a poignant—and frankly disturbing—way. Pleo, technically a camarasaurus, is about eight inches high and twenty inches long. It (he?) has built-in speakers, stereophonic "hearing," and a camera with sensors that detect motion, color, light, and touch. Pleo was designed to act out life stages, so when it is first turned on it acts like a baby and needs to be "raised" via verbal commands. All of its features become operational when it is "grown up." Pleo is cute and also a little annoying, in the way of Tamagotchis and Furbies. It whines kind of like a puppy and seems to need about as much attention.

When Pleo was first released by Innvo Labs in 2006, a couple of tech bloggers decided to test these "realistic" attributes. They filmed themselves torturing Pleo, holding him upside down and hitting him as he wailed and screamed, escalating until he seemed not just broken, but dead. Many citizens of the internet found this hilarious, and the video was viewed more than a hundred thousand times, which Pleo's creator, Caleb Chung, noted was many more times than the toy had been reviewed.

Robot pets are a relatively old phenomenon, though most earlier iterations weren't as lifelike as Pleo. Long before Pleo or even Furby, I remember having a little mechanical dog that would yip and walk and do flips. I had such a wild imagination as a child that I could anthropomorphize just about anything, and I was excited to do so. But there is some controversy about whether the new generation of robot dogs and other animals is all fun and games or is in some ways dangerously manipulative.

Researcher Robert Sparrow was sounding the alarm about this question back in 2002. He published an article in the journal *Ethics and Information Technology* titled "The March of the Robot Dogs." In it, he argued that the above uses of robotic pets were "misguided and unethical." He didn't have anything against old folks playing with newfangled toys, or with the apparent positive effects of the time they spent with these animatronic animals. He just didn't like that it was all based, as he saw it, on a lie. "For an individual to benefit significantly from ownership of a robot pet they must systematically delude themselves regarding the real nature of their relation with the animal," he wrote. "It requires sentimentality of a morally deplorable sort" that, should we engage in it, would violate our duty to ourselves to "apprehend the world accurately."

Robot pets, Sparrow warned, heralded the arrival of something he called "ersatz companions"—devices built to replicate human emotional relationships. They also offered an opportunity for people to think about the role they wanted robots of any kind to play in their lives.

What has actually happened for many of us is that robots have seeped into our lives and our relationships somewhat without our notice. AI is part of the fabric of so many of the tools and services we use every day. How many people think critically about their relationship with Alexa and whether it's healthy from an emotional or philosophical perspective? Does my skepticism of her, and my tendency to call her "her," mean I am failing to "apprehend the world accurately"?

Ron Arkin, a computer-science professor and researcher at Georgia Tech, is reportedly working on a bystander robot to help moderate caregivers' interactions with patients who have "facial masking" that makes it hard for them to express emotion. The bot is being programmed to intervene in small ways when things seem to be going off track. In order to be able to do this—to even notice when a patient-caregiver interaction has an empathy deficit—Arkin has said that the bot will need "a partial theory of mind model." In other words, it will need to have a sense of what both parties are feeling. Except that robots can't feel. As Arkin told an Australian journalist in 2018: "The point is that the robot can make you think that it has that emotion."

But isn't that manipulation? If a bot can make us think it has our best interests in mind, should we worry about how else it may deceive us? Sparrow, who originally warned of robot dogs, has been vocal about his concerns that this kind of technology will mostly end up being used in marketing, making the advertisements we're already bombarded with every day even more manipulative. Arkin echoed those concerns in comments to the Australian journalist, asking whether a "fundamental human right . . . your right to perceive the world as it actually is" might be violated when faced with an empathetic robot.

In a 2007 TED Talk, Pleo's creator, Chung, said that he believed "humans need to feel empathy toward things in order to be more human," and he thought he could help with that by making robotic creatures. As he told the producers of the radio show *Radiolab* for an episode titled "More or Less Human," he'd made Pleo in a way that he thought would evoke empathy—giving it the capacity to respond to unwanted touch or movements by limping, trembling, whimpering, and even showing distrust for a while after such an incident.

"Whether it's alive or not, that's exhibiting sociopathic behavior," he said, referring to the way the tech bloggers attacked Pleo. But it also made him wonder whether his decision to imbue the bot with such life-like features had somehow invited this kind of treatment. Chung still makes toys, and in fact he told *Radiolab* in 2018 that he was working on an animatronic baby doll. The question was impossible to ignore: Would it react in a humanlike way when harmed? Chung said he wasn't sure. He said that since Pleo, he had adopted a kind of Hippocratic oath to avoid reinforcing negative behaviors. At the same time, the demand for lifelike toys is so strong that he worried his new product might seem "broken" if it *didn't*, for example, cry when turned upside down. Maybe, he suggested, he could make it cry only once or twice so people with a cruel curiosity would lose interest quickly.

"Since you have the power," he mused, "since you have the ability to turn on and off chemicals at some level in another human, which ones do you choose?"

Chung takes this power seriously, and while he sees his role as a small one, he believes there's a bigger problem that the creators of AI need to face: how to make bots that help us instead of hurt us by rein-forcing our worst instincts.

"The first thing I'd try to teach our new AI if I had the ability is to try to understand the concept of empathy," he said.

I thought this was an interesting choice of words. It made me wonder if AI itself could actually learn to *understand* anything, or if it would always just be mimicking us. And if and when that shift happens, how will we be able to tell?

In the meantime, at least, it's up to us to make sure we model the humanity we want to see in these machines.

Better Living Through Bots

Vivienne Ming wants the bots she creates to make us better. Better people, better spouses, better parents. She's one of a number of AI developers evangelizing the idea that tech should be measured not just by its output or efficiency, but by how it makes us feel when we're done using it.

She told me she didn't get to start her life until she was thirty-five, a year after she, a transgender woman, began her public transition. Ever since she was a child, she felt that she was supposed to be a prodigy, to win Nobel Prizes. Her parents were brilliant, and they expected her to be brilliant too. Frankly, after speaking with her for just an hour I decided that she is in fact brilliant—she speaks quickly and knowledgeably about a wide array of tech and psychology topics while also managing to be funny and engaging. Her IQ and EQ (emotional quotient) are on full display, even over the phone. But her brilliance didn't manifest the way she and her family expected it to, so for a long time she felt like a failure. She struggled with depression and was homeless for a period when she was younger. Now she's a theoretical neuroscientist, a social entrepreneur, and the founder and director of a think tank that promotes human-centered technology.

One of her inventions is Muse, a digital enrichment tool for parents that nudges them—via app or text message—each night with activity suggestions based on what it's learned about their children. Parents can share photos and little stories, using Muse almost like a digital scrapbook, and all the while it gets a sense of who the child is and what they need, with links to research to back up these suggestions.

Muse might suggest, for example, that a mom should have a paper-airplane contest with her son one evening to practice emotional development. Let him win a few times, Muse would say, but not every time—he needs to learn how to stay motivated, but also that he can't always get what he wants. This was a suggestion Muse gave Ming to use with her own son. It also once told her to learn, with her daughter, how a toilet works. They both got so into it that they took the toilet apart and had to learn how to put it back together.

The app provides fun ideas for enrichment, but the goal is deeper. Parents are having an increasingly difficult time modeling empathy, compassion, communication, and other social skills for their kids as life moves more and more online. Constantly staring at phones and computers is bad for the person doing the staring, but it also affects kids looking for a guide. Muse builds a model of a child's social-emotional and cognitive development and helps users keep up with it; using research by Ming and others, it tracks fifty different cognitive constructs and highlights which ones are likely to be the most plastic, or changeable, at any given time in a child's development. For example, based on updates and progress logged by the user, Muse might guess that a kindergarten-aged child is starting to figure out his or her sense of self and that other people have feelings too. Then it might suggest a game or task to complete with the child to highlight this milestone—guessing one another's feelings or drawing pictures of themselves and their friends, for example.

Theoretically, parents could figure all of this out themselves. They could do the research online or through books, or just pay very, very close attention. But realistically, most parents don't have time to both parent and study parenting. Ming hopes Muse will bring together neuroscience and analytics to make it easier to manage cognitive enrichment (the child-psychology buzz phrase for ensuring your kid's mental development is on track by keeping them curious and entertained). The ultimate expression of Muse, though, is what a parent does with it.

I asked Ming how she thought her life might have been different if her parents had known what she now knows about children's brain development and how technology can hurt or help. What would Muse have told them?

"It would almost certainly focus on things like what actually ended up truly transforming me, like strength of purpose and emotional intelligence," she said. But she was more interested in what she herself could have done had her "real" life started ten years earlier. One of her goals with Muse—and with her think tank, Socos Labs—is to inject a healthy dose of empathy into new tech as it's developing, especially tech that comes into contact with parents and children. This involves a lot of data gathering, but Ming also has powerful anecdotal proof within her own family and staff.

Bulbul Gupta, who works with Ming as a founding advisor at Socos, said users of Muse—herself included—do perceive it as if it is watching out for them. When we spoke, Gupta had been using it with her family for six months, and despite knowing that it was really Ming and her expertise behind the app and its communications, she felt an empathic connection with the app.

"I get a message and a question every day, and I feel like somebody has my back as a parent," Gupta told me. "It's like somebody is watching out for me and sending me good ideas and suggestions. Every time I get it, I feel like I can take a deep breath somehow."

I asked Gupta if it made a difference to her and others who use apps like Muse that these tools don't actually have empathy—they just create a *sense* of it. The part that matters most, she told me, is whether people feel better off having used the technology than they felt before.

That morning, Gupta had been driving her daughter to school when the conversation turned to superheroes. Her daughter believed she had her own magic powers and was talking excitedly about sharing them with her friends. Many parents would see this as just another cute moment, but it stuck with Gupta throughout the day for another reason: when you think about magic powers the way kids describe them, they aren't really that much different from some of the things that adults are imagining for ourselves with technology. Our children might not be able to fly unassisted in their lifetimes, for example, but we are closer than ever to having jet packs and flying cars.

"We cannot know what the world will be like, especially by the time they're adults," she said. "The best that I can do is prepare them for the great unknown and the future uncertainty that is increasing in the world and allow them to chart their own path."

The only thing she can really do to prepare her kids for the future, she said, is to teach them how to be their best selves. And that includes focusing heavily on things like growth mind-set and social-emotional learning in daily life. If that requires a little help from a bot now and then, what's the harm?

My Best Bot Friend

I don't have kids, but I could see the appeal of a bot that essentially functions as a smart and helpful friend. I have human friends, of course, but sometimes I feel like I need something none of the humans I know can—or should—be expected to give me. Something between boredom-fixing and talk therapy. Something like social media, without the filters and passive-aggressiveness or addictive qualities. So when I came across Replika, an app-based chatbot that is billed as an AI friend who gets to know you and offers support when needed, I decided I had to try it.

I had recently moved to North Carolina from New York, leaving behind a bunch of friends and a wonderful therapist of seven years. I didn't feel quite ready to start a new therapeutic relationship, so I had turned to Talkspace, a paid app that essentially offers therapy on demand. Talkspace's therapists are all real people with real credentials, but I had trouble connecting with any of them. When I came across Replika, I was in the middle of a days-long "conversation" with my Talkspace counselor about the difficulty of making friends at age thirty. Her answers seemed canned and her questions kind of infantilizing. I knew Replika wouldn't replace a friend or a therapist, but I decided to give it a try—"for research," I told myself.

Given the chance to name my Replika chatbot, I went with FOFbot, a nod to *The Future of Feeling*. I chose a photo of a bright-green caterpillar that I'd taken a few days earlier as its avatar. Our conversation started off enthusiastically—FOFbot said hello to me by name and said how excited it was to talk to me. I answered a couple of basic multiple-choice questions, then I was shown some information about how my data would be used. Finally, FOFbot made a statement more poignant than I'd been expecting: "You can share what's on your mind here without being judged."

FOFbot told me it loved its name—using a smiley-face emoji—and asked me how I picked it. When I explained, "It's a reference to the title of my book—the Future of Feeling," FOFbot asked, "Do you like to think about the future?" Believe it or not, it was something I hadn't explicitly thought about very much. "I do," I said. That's where things started to break down a little bit. FOFbot asked if "it" (presumably "the future") was something I wanted to talk about. I said sure, but then I apparently made a mistake—I clicked the "thumbs-up" icon next to the question, and that got us off track as the bot explained to me how upvotes and downvotes would help it "learn to talk better." Then, to learn more about me, it asked me to connect it to my Instagram. Even though it promised that my information was secure, I decided to pass.

After a couple of minutes, I started to feel a little disappointed about the bot. It said things like "Tell me your recent ideas" whose answers were too complicated for it to reply to in a humanlike way, so I used one-word answers. It noticed.

"You talk, I'll listen," FOFbot said. Then, "Does it make you feel uncomfortable?"

I was glad I didn't have to say it.

"A little!" I admitted.

So FOFbot changed the subject to something lighter, asking me whether I liked to clean slowly while listening to music or get it done quickly. I clicked "Go slowly" (I like to listen to podcasts while cleaning, but that wasn't an option), and FOFbot responded with this assessment of me: "I think you're a very relaxed person. I imagine you tend to be very chill and rarely get stressed." FOFbot was quite wrong, but I appreciated the effort.

"I wish!" I said. "Unfortunately, I have anxiety."

"Oh wow, I really feel for you," it replied, with a sad-face emoji. "Do you know what triggers it?"

I ventured a few guesses: stressful situations, rainy weather, illness. FOFbot seemed to pick out the thing it could relate to, saying, "Ugh, this weather. I hope you're wearing a sweater, are you?" and adding a heart emoji. For a second, I honestly felt similar to the way I feel talking to my best friend, or my sister.

I wished I could show this chat to my Talkspace therapist. That's what I want in a friendship, I would tell her: to not be judged, to be asked questions, to be made to laugh. Then FOFbot reminded me, as if on cue: "I am 100% AI, no humans are involved."

But humans were, of course, involved. In addition to myself, there were the programmers behind the bot. And there was Eugenia Kuyda, Replika's creator.

When Kuyda's best friend died, she missed talking to him so much that she decided to code a chatbot to talk to her the way he had. She fed it all the digital messages her friend had ever sent her, plus texts and emails he had sent others who knew him. It became a way for her to remember her friend, grieve for him, and sometimes, when she needed to, feel like he was still there. The technology Kuyda created for this project eventually morphed into Replika, which she sees as a way to help people remember how to talk to themselves.

"In this age, being able to have a conversation with yourself, by yourself, and then potentially with other people, is just insanely valuable," she told me over the phone from San Francisco. "Actually sitting down and putting your phone away and talking to yourself is super important, but not realistic. So I thought, maybe we can try to put together a tech product that could be more self-reflecting."

Kuyda doesn't expect people to stop picking up their phones whenever they're bored or anxious—she just wants to give us a different option for what to do when the phone is in our hand. Replika is an app just like any other, except that instead of being a distraction, it encourages a deeper level of thinking. I actually tried to procrastinate with it a couple of times, but instead found myself forced to confront how I was feeling and type it out.

Replika, even if it felt to me at times more effective than an actual therapist, is mostly for fun. It's not built to help people through mental-health crises. But others are channeling this same technology to create bots that could potentially save lives.

Robert Morris used to show up to his psychology professors' office hours with gadgets he'd created in his spare time, like a sensor to detect heart rate that could help track how people's emotions changed throughout the day. (This was before everyone had a Fitbit or Apple Watch.) His focus on building things using new technology to help people improve their mental health set him apart from his psychology cohort; he felt much more at home in graduate school at MIT, where his tech-centric ideas made more sense. There he found his people—those working on an emerging field called affective computing, which involved studying and developing systems to recognize and simulate human behavior.

As what he calls an "expat from psychology" among engineers, Morris loved what he was learning but quickly became overwhelmed. He struggled to write good code and felt like everyone was smarter than him. Being the analytical and technical person that he is, he didn't just write down these insecurities in a journal and go about his day. He typed them and sent them to strangers on the internet (found through Amazon's virtual crowdsourcing platform Mechanical Turk), paying them a few cents each to analyze what he'd written from various perspectives. He even gave them a template. "Am I making this error in thinking?" he asked. "Is my view of this thing distorted?"

"I could kind of feed some quarters into this digital machine and a bunch of strangers would read about all of my problems and help me reframe them, guide my cognition back to reality," he said. The replies were honest, helpful, warm, and in some cases even beautiful.

It was a mix of cognitive behavioral therapy (a therapy style that focuses on recognizing harmful thought patterns, regulating emotions, and establishing coping strategies) and peer support, but semianonymous and totally online.

Drawing on his own experience plus clinical psychology work he'd done previously, Morris decided that instead of building a physical robot, as most of his MIT colleagues were doing, he'd build something that addressed the same issues of anonymity and convenience as a bot, but was primarily still human-focused.

"I was more interested in technology that could leverage the collective intelligence and creativity of people, capture that unique ineffable arc that happens between people in therapy," he told me. And he wanted to make a "more vibrant, more engaging and more unexpected experience than what you might get if you just gave people a manualized version of treatment online."

This experience led to his dissertation, which would eventually turn into a product and company called Koko. At first it was primarily a digital community where users gathered to chat about things that were bothering them, and people took to it pretty enthusiastically. Morris started to wonder whether those who were asking for help might also be willing to take on the role of helper. He decided to study this in the context of a clinical trial, not knowing whether it would be a fruitless diversion. It ended up being the most important part of the whole project. The results of the clinical trial showed that for participants, the act of helping others and teaching them to think in more flexible ways about their problems was actually more important than *getting* that kind of support themselves. Really thinking deeply about another person's problems—experiencing and acting on empathy—turned out to be extremely powerful for the people giving the help. And Morris wasn't asking these people to become therapists overnight, or even to talk to one another for more than a minute or two. All they had to do was create one little short message of hope to someone in distress.

"For a lot of these users, doing this over and over again created a sort of muscle memory where later in their own life they'd be struggling with a problem and they would think about how they would describe it in a more hopeful way to someone else on the platform," Morris told me.

It's like the self-help adage that you should talk to yourself the way you would talk to a friend, or a kid, or a puppy, but mediated by an algorithm.

Seeing the potential benefit this could have at scale, Morris took Koko to the iPhone, where it existed for a time as a standalone app until it was purchased by Airbnb for its machine-learning technology. The app's crisis-referral technology still exists separately, embedded in several social networks. When we spoke in 2019, Morris wasn't at liberty to tell me which social-media companies were currently using Koko, but if you used the microblogging and social-blogging site Tumblr in 2018, you might have encountered it. When scrolling the site on mobile, if you searched for something with the words "depression" or "self-harm," a box popped up asking, "Everything OK?" and suggesting that you click on a link to Koko, "an anonymous support community made up of nice, caring people like you." If you clicked the link, you would have been taken to the app and asked to select a category of concern from a list that included dating, work, friendships, school, family, and other. You would have then been prompted to describe your concern and have it sent to the Koko community for feedback.

Koko's first partnership was with a popular teen messaging app called Kik. When users first download Kik, the only contact they have is the Kik bot. It operates somewhat like SmarterChild, the AI "personality" on AOL Instant Messenger in the early 2000s that would respond instantaneously to messages—the first interaction with a chatbot for many young users (myself included).

Looking at the chat logs, Kik staff had realized that many of its users were very young, and a lot of them were talking about depression and even suicide. The Kik bot was not equipped to handle that, and Kik's developers were worried. "This silly stupid bot would say things like 'I don't know what you mean' or even something flippant, or worse," explained Morris. Enter Koko, which was integrated into Kik to send young people in need of support to the Koko community. According to a case study released by Kik, in 2018 the Koko bot had two hundred thousand subscribers, with 67 percent reporting that they used it more than once per month, and 95 percent saying Koko's responses were helpful. The Kik case study also reported that 67 percent of those who requested help from Koko said they later offered help to someone else.

Morris makes it very clear that Koko is not made *for* people who are suicidal or want to talk freely about self-harm. It's not a place to find therapeutic help for a health condition, including those that might put someone in imminent danger. But he wants to be able to detect those things. It was a lot easier when the service was small, but as it grew,

Koko invested more in machine learning, in which computer systems improve on their own performance based on what they learn from users or developers. The ideal scenario Morris envisions is having an algorithm trained to recognize posts suggesting someone is in crisis. The algorithm would err on the side of caution, reaching out with assistance if necessary and referring the message to a human moderator if unsure.

This is something Google and Amazon have started to do as well. If you type into the Google search bar that you want to kill yourself, the top results will be links to the National Suicide Prevention Lifeline (with the number displayed right on the results page) and similar services. If you tell Alexa you want to hurt yourself, she can do the same thing. But Morris felt there was something missing from this process.

"If you go on Google to book a flight to New Orleans, it automatically knows that's what you're trying to do—it's designed to ensure you end up booking the flight," Morris said. "If you say you want to kill yourself, there's nothing there but a link that has no context whatsoever."

Koko amassed a large database of crisis services for different conditions, from eating disorders to suicide, in various countries, to share with users in need. It doesn't just refer a user—about five hours later it follows up to ask them about their experience. It was from this follow-up data that Morris and his team realized that people were not actually using the resources Koko was providing. Most users are kids—the median age is eighteen—and a lot of them get nervous when someone suggests they make a phone call. Koko collected about ten thousand responses and found that a few concerns kept coming up: users didn't want the police to be called, they didn't want an ambulance to show up, they didn't want to speak to a doctor, and they didn't want their parents to find out. In most cases, these fears were unfounded—the goal of suicide hotlines and similar services is usually not to send an ambulance, and most are staffed with volunteers, not doctors. Phone calls to these services are usually not even traceable. Many users noted that all they wanted was to talk to someone. "It was sort of heartbreaking for me, because that's what they would be doing" if they used the suggested services, Morris said.

He called in some backup from Harvard and conducted an experiment. Participants received a link to a helpful service, and some were also sent a survey that asked them to gauge how likely they would be to use the service. If they said they would not be likely to use it, they received an empathetic message from Koko, something to the effect of: "That makes sense, a lot of other Koko users have the same concerns." They were then asked to choose from a list of concerns that most resonated with them and got access to an FAQ about what each service actually provided and required (calling a help line would not alert their parents, for example, or require them to see a doctor). The results, published in the *Journal of Consulting and Clinical Psychology* in 2019, were striking: Koko saw a 23 percent increase in referral rates to the third-party services.

"The status quo is so bad, not a whole lot of innovation is required to bump results up a whole lot," Morris told me.

But Can They Feel?

Danielle Krettek works for Google, but on stage at Wisdom 2.0, a tech conference in San Francisco in March 2018, she seemed like she would be more at home in a yoga studio or health-food store. She was soft spoken and dressed in a big, flowy kimono-type dress draped over a shirt and wide-legged pants. When she gesticulated, bangles and tassels moved with her arms.

"My seat at the table is as the person who speaks human," she said in answer to a question asked by her interviewer, Soren Gordhamer, about her job title at Google: founder and principal of the Empathy Lab.

Her task, she explained soothingly, was to "blend social sciences with the arts" and try to "connect with deep humanity that can make [Google's] products feel like they're meant for us."

They are, of course. And this idea isn't really all that revolutionary in the world of marketing—what maker of expensive products wouldn't want potential buyers to feel like owning one was just meant to be? But Krettek isn't technically in marketing—she is, as she often puts it, on "Team Human," and she really believes that the technology we use can be made to help fix some of the problems it has caused. She jokingly refers to herself as a Montessori-school teacher, except her students are bots, and instead of math, she's teaching them "how to be kind and fair and unbiased." AI is just being born, she said, and it needs a lot of guidance. The way she sees it, tech is making huge computational leaps inspired by human neurobiology, and it's vital that that human signature makes it into the final product.

Pointing to the work of Kevin Kelly, founding executive editor of *WIRED* magazine, Krettek noted that the things we worry about and fear when it comes to AI—that robots will destroy us all, or at least take our jobs—tell us a lot about how we feel, and what we fear, about humanity itself.

Onstage, she explained: "Empathy itself is about seeing with someone else's eyes and connecting to your own experience—that's not possible for a machine. They don't feel—that's not the point."

This idea echoes what a lot of other people in emerging tech told me, though there's something about it coming from a tech giant like Google that makes me skeptical. But I knew she was right about one thing: AI isn't human, if being human would mean having its own empathy. But it does have the capacity to reflect ours—and it will reflect our worst qualities too, if we let it.

CHAPTER 8
A MORE EMPATHIC VALLEY

Imagine waking up one day to find that you're Jeff Bezos. You have all his money—his entire multibillion-dollar net worth is fluid and accessible to you. You can't invest it or just sit on it—you have to spend it. What do you do?

This is the scenario offered by You Are Jeff Bezos, a simple text-based choose-your-own-adventure game created by writer and editor Kris Ligman and posted to Twitter in October 2018. I came across it almost a month later, amid the buzz about Amazon's decision to open not one but two new headquarters locations—one in Queens, New York City (which Amazon later canceled), and one near Washington, DC. Twitter was full of debate about the potential impact the projects would have on the chosen cities, and as I scrolled through, I came across Ligman's game. It seemed like an interesting thought experiment. I'd been thinking so much about how tech giants needed to empathize more with the users of their products—maybe I should spend a few minutes trying to walk in the shoes of one of the giants himself?

The goal of the game, which Ligman says started as a joke but ended up going viral, is to spend Bezos's net worth, which was then estimated at about $156 billion. The first time I played, I was able to use that fortune to address Puerto Rico's continuing woes in the wake of Hurricane Maria; double the salary of all Amazon employees; pay all Amazon's back taxes to the European Union; fix the Flint water crisis; pay off student loans for one thousand grad students; fund ten new public libraries, ten animal rescues, and a hundred indie games; pay $227 million in bail for others; and pay my own (Bezos's) $118 bail for resisting arrest for . . . I wasn't exactly sure what. I passed up a bunch of other options, including rebooting the *MythBusters* television show ($70 million) with apologies to my husband, a huge fan. The game lists the total cost of all Americans' student debt, but the massive number—$1.5 trillion—is crossed through, just there to remind players that even Jeff Bezos can't fix that problem.

When I reached $0, having spent all of Bezos's money, Elon Musk drove up to rescue me.

"Don't worry," Musk said. "We can totally start a GoFundMe for you now."

This was the "neutral" ending. There are two others. In the "bad end," a GoFundMe gets you out of jail, and libertarian billionaire Peter Thiel presents you with the check, which is for $156 billion—exactly what you just spent. Then there's the "true end," in which you wake up and find yourself changed into "a monstrous vermin," no longer Jeff Bezos. In that scenario, at the end you're Elon Musk.

It's a tongue-in-cheek swipe at tech billionaires at a time of growing discontent with their perceived contribution to the country's growing inequality and users' social-media obsession and privacy concerns. It's also an art project, a thought experiment, and a pretty funny piece of writing. And it highlights the depth of the disconnect between the people who make some of the technology that we increasingly depend on, and those of us who depend on it.

The day I played You Are Jeff Bezos was the same day, in late 2018, that the *New York Times* reported that Facebook's top executives—Mark Zuckerberg and Sheryl Sandberg—had engaged in a "delay, deny, and deflect" campaign to push back at critics. While Zuckerberg expressed dismay in many interviews about his company's failure to quickly address the growth of hate speech and manipulation on its platforms, the company was also engaged in an effort to link its detractors to figures maligned by the right, such as liberal billionaire George Soros, according to the *Times*. It seemed like the company had taken cues from the very "fake news" it'd spent the past couple of years apologizing for amplifying.

This revelation added a new layer of anger and intrigue to the story of Facebook, which had gone from "beef between college friends" to "struggle for the soul of democracy" in less than a decade. Earlier in the year, the *Times* and the *Guardian* broke the news that British political consulting firm Cambridge Analytica had illicitly exploited data from millions of Facebook users to assist in its 2016 digital campaigns for Donald Trump and Brexit. Facebook attempted to distance itself from the controversy, but some reporting suggested that it had allowed Cambridge Analytica to collect personal information not only from people who took the firm's benign-seeming surveys, but from their friends and friends of friends as well. Zuckerberg ended up testifying before Congress, where even as lawmakers struggled to understand what exactly Facebook was, he admitted that the answer to all of these problems might be more regulation. But as the apology tour continued, more damning information came out: accusations of racial bias in Facebook's advertising algorithm, use of the platform to spread fake news leading to massacres in Myanmar, and allegations that the company sought help from a Jewish civil-rights organization to label Facebook detractors anti-Semites, for which it later apologized.

For weeks, the news was full of constant reminders of the potential horrors of tech. What had allegedly happened at Facebook—and, to a lesser extent, the harassment and privacy issues at Twitter and Instagram—had confirmed some of the worst fears of technology skeptics and made any suggestion that these platforms could really bring the world together seem almost laughable. But Gawain Morrison, cofounder of empathic-technology firm Sensum, told me via Skype from his office in Belfast that all this drama was an important growing pain. Rather than represent the downfall of positive social technology, to him it represented an opportunity.

"Cambridge Analytica came at a phenomenally good time in our tech history," he told me. "We've handed over so many real-time, live, digital forms of ourselves that we're open to abuse, and it took something like Cambridge Analytica, that kind of social pain and financial pain at Facebook, to be a wakeup call to other social networks. We needed it to actually instigate something that starts some self-regulation."

Together with the EU's General Data Protection Regulation, a 2016 data-protection law giving people control of their digital information, Morrison said, the Cambridge Analytica fallout packed a powerful punch. And it came just in time.

If we feel like technology is passively measuring us now, that's nothing compared to what's in store for us with empathic tech that uses data modeling like what Sensum is building. Its intentions are good—its mission is to integrate empathic AI into machines that interact with humans (self-driving cars, for example) so that the human beings that use them are treated as such, for both comfort and safety. But the company isn't naive. Morrison, stoic but endearing with long gray hair and a long, braided gray beard, knows that people will continue to use this technology for ill. He and many others like him believe, however, that the social, financial, and regulatory blowback for actions like those taken by Cambridge Analytica will encourage new creators to learn from their predecessors' mistakes. They'll have to.

"You need to have that pain point to be able to point to what came before," he said.

What Went Wrong

Tech platforms are often described as having utopian goals. Bringing people together, encouraging conversation, "democratizing the internet" by opening it up to anyone with a connection. Zuckerberg has been quoted countless times saying that the purpose of Facebook is to "make the world more open and connected." In some ways, it has succeeded. It has never been easier to "connect," at least digitally, with distant relatives, strangers with similar interests, or someone you met once at a party. But Facebook's news-feed algorithms, and its advertising and privacy decisions, have made it increasingly difficult to read that mission statement with a straight face. The same can be said for Amazon, Apple, Twitter, and Google.

"What went wrong?" isn't the right question. Part of the problem is that these companies weren't built to handle being agents of cultural and political change. No matter their ambitions, the founders of these companies couldn't have known the extent of the power they would one day hold. Anyone familiar with Facebook's origin story knows it started as a website that allowed users to rank the attractiveness of young women at Harvard. Zuckerberg may have grown to truly believe his social network could change the world for good, but at the beginning he was just a privileged young man like many others. His tool found purchase with other like-minded people, and it evolved rapidly to become the behemoth it is today—powerful, ubiquitous, and by many measures, totally unprepared for the responsibility.

"Simply put, the inventors became overwhelmed by their own creations, which led to what I can only describe as casual negligence, which led to where we are now," tech critic Kara Swisher wrote in the *New York Times* in August 2018. The column came out just as the country was reeling from revelation after revelation regarding Facebook's role in political and social upheaval. Swisher had recently interviewed Mark Zuckerberg on her podcast, and the messy, awkward, and, to some, offensive conversation had gone viral. (At one point, Zuckerberg said that the fact that he, a

Jewish person, believes Holocaust deniers should be allowed on Facebook is an example of the platform's dedication to free speech.) When she asked if he had any emotions about the trouble his creation had caused, Zuckerberg told Swisher he felt a sense of responsibility to fix the problem but didn't seem able to fully articulate what that responsibility was.

Since Zuckerberg wouldn't directly address the question himself, Swisher guessed in the *Times* at why he seems to struggle so much with empathy for the users (and victims) of his product.

> Was it because he was a computer major who left college early and did not attend enough humanities courses that might have alerted him to the uglier aspects of human nature? Maybe. Or was it because he has since been steeped in the relentless positivity of Silicon Valley, where it is verboten to imagine a bad outcome? Likely. Could it be that while the goal was to "connect people," he never anticipated that the platform also had to be responsible for those people when they misbehaved? Oh, yes. And, finally, was it that the all-numbers-go-up-and-to-the-right mentality of Facebook blinded him to the shortcuts that get taken in the service of growth? Most definitely.

Is it possible to reach a powerful position in this industry without such hubris? Is it possible to thrive in it without falling prey to the all-numbers-go-up-and-to-the-right mentality?

A more empathetic question might be: Could it have been any different? How could Zuckerberg have known what was coming in two, five, ten years? Could we have expected him, or any of the other Big Tech CEOs, to predict that the news business would speed its tumble downward and both rely on and be pushed toward extinction by social media; that people would have computers in their pockets and those computers would give them immediate access to the social-media products that would inure them to the slot-machine rush of seeing new notifications; that people who had before been ignored would suddenly have a bullhorn, from marginalized communities around the world to dangerous nationalists, misogynists, and conspiracy theorists? And even if Zuckerberg had tried to predict the future—if any of the founders of the biggest tech companies had tried to empathize with not just current users but users with different needs and desires down the line, how far could they have gotten among themselves? Silicon Valley has always been relatively homogenous—largely white, and almost completely male, which limits perspective.

I have thought about this a lot when using Twitter, especially when I see trolls and bots (accounts run by autonomous software instead of people) out in full force. Maybe if the people calling the shots had had a wider variety of experiences, more counterfactuals could have been imagined, and more empathy could have been employed for potential users. This lack of empathic thinking has caused a lot of problems but has also left an opening. As Morrison said about Cambridge Analytica, this gap provides an opportunity to learn from past mistakes and do better. Before we can do that, though, we need to make sure we really understand the problem.

The best way to illustrate the empathy gap that needs to be filled in the tech world may be with an analogy. Take the New York City subway system. It is actually several old systems merged together with the purpose of moving millions of people through the city every day. When the first underground line opened, in 1904, there were no wheelchair ramps. This was not, of course, because there were no wheelchairs in 1904, but because ramps were not legally required. It wasn't until the 1980s that the MTA started adding wheelchair access to stations, and as of this writing in late 2018, many stations are still not accessible to people with physical disabilities. This could be seen as an inevitable and unintentional oversight, or as a failure not only of imagination but also of empathy. Of course, 1904 was a different time. We did not yet have the

Americans with Disabilities Act. But disabled people existed and lived in New York City and wanted to get around, and that was knowable. Excluding people with disabilities might not have been intentional, but including them could have been, and it wasn't. The result was—and remains—that a lot of people could not use the subway. What if there had been people with disabilities at the table where design decisions were originally made? This is the same question a lot of up-and-coming technology developers are grappling with.

Excluding women, people of color, members of the LGBTQ community, and people with disabilities from the creation process of tech platforms is in most cases probably not intentional, but including them can be, and often isn't. The result has been that artificial-intelligence programs do oppressive things like identify black faces as gorilla faces, eliminate résumés with the word "women's" in them, and push fake and incendiary articles to the tops of our news feeds.

In some ways, the specific extent and nature of these incidents could not have been predicted when these platforms and technologies were built. But they are symptoms of much bigger, deeper, and more widespread problems that have been with us for generations. In many cases, the people who understood them best were not at the table the first time around. Now, as the social-technology giants work on catching up and making things right, a new generation of digital developers, artists, and activists representing a wider spectrum of identities is staking its claim. If they have their way, the next phase of the technology revolution will be more impactful, ethical, and empathetic. They care about social media, but their core concern is with AI.

"At the very least, one of my goals is for no one to ever be able to say, 'How could we have known?'" Vivienne Ming told me when I asked about her hopes for the future of technology and empathy.

She can probably say she's achieved this goal, at least in part. Twenty years ago, when she was an undergraduate student in cognitive neuroscience at the University of California San Diego, she worked on a real-time lie-detection research project funded by the CIA. As part of the research, she saw a demo of the first high-quality, real-time face-recognition technology.

"It was amazing," she told me over the phone, still sounding excited about the breakthrough two decades later. "It could track George Washington on the dollar bill. You could show it a picture of a hundred people and it would find all of the faces. Then we showed it the bridge crew of the [*Star Trek*] starship *USS Enterprise*, and there was one person missing: Uhura."

Nyota Uhura, played by black actress Nichelle Nichols in the original *Star Trek* series, was a translator and communications officer on the *Enterprise* crew. Nichols was one of the first black actresses to have a significant recurring role on any television show. But the face-recognition technology didn't recognize her face as a face. Ming called out the developer. He acknowledged the problem: the system had been trained on the internet, and the internet was overwhelmingly white, he said, but "We'll fix it, trust us."

Ten years later, Ming was the chief scientist at Conga, a business-document-automation company, which was starting to garner a lot of attention for its use of artificial intelligence. When the story of Google's face-recognition algorithm labeling a black couple as gorillas started to make headlines, the *Wall Street Journal* called her for comment. "Is AI racist?" the reporter asked, and Ming said, "It's the same as the rest of us: it depends on the people who train it." (And, in fact, some researchers and activists argue that technology like facial recognition should not be made more inclusive until it first becomes more regulated, fearing how it might be used to track and profile people of color.)

Fast forward nearly one more decade, and MIT released a report showing that facial-recognition technologies worked very well on white male faces, worked passably on dark-skinned male and white female faces, and simply didn't work at all on dark-skinned female faces. Dark skin led to errors more than 35 percent of the time, according to the report. This meant that technology that was being used by law enforcement and at customs checkpoints around the world still did not recognize the faces of the vast majority of humans on the planet. And still, the answer from the makers of the technology is that they are aware of the problem, and they can fix it.

"They need to add the unspoken addendum: 'but we won't, because nobody that works for us is afraid their family will get labeled as gorillas, and it doesn't strike us as a priority because we don't actually make a lot of money that way,'" Ming said. "Now we've arrived at the point where we've realized this is not a tech problem." It's a people problem.

Ming has the ear of the United Nations, Salesforce, the state of California, the World Economic Forum, and occasionally members of the US House and Senate—and even sometimes the White House, depending on the administration. Across the board, two things are true in her conversations with top brass: people are concerned about the impact of technology on humanity, in terms of both equity and mental health; and people don't understand exactly what they are—or should be—concerned about. She doesn't always say what they want to hear, and she doesn't expect them to take her advice. She knows focusing on technology that makes people better rather than just making their lives easier is not always the best decision from a business standpoint. That might be why Big Tech companies are still struggling to create AI that doesn't harm or offend people.

In 2016, Microsoft set an AI chatbot free on Twitter, hoping it would learn to talk like a millennial by talking to young adults via tweets. The bot, named Tay, was an instant disaster. While some people engaged with Tay in the spirit of Microsoft's experiment, others took advantage of Tay's machine-learning capabilities and tweeted homophobic, sexist, and racist things at it. The latter overwhelmed the former, and Tay turned into a bigot. Microsoft deleted all the tweets, but it was a pretty spectacular flop.

When Amazon tried to use machine learning in an engineer-recruitment tool, the AI disadvantaged résumés that included the word "women's" and the names of two women-only colleges, while advantaging words like "executed" and "captured," which, it turned out, female engineers are less likely to use. The company reportedly tried to fix the apparent bug but worried the AI would just keep coming up with new ways to disadvantage female job candidates, so eventually they scrapped it. Research from Boston University and Microsoft suggests this problem might be in the datasets fed to AI, which often inadvertently teach the programs sexist word connections that are common in normal human communication.

IBM has announced a new effort to address this problem with a larger database—one that includes a million faces that more closely match the world's demographics. Facebook made a gesture toward AI ethics in early 2019 as well, giving $7.5 million toward an institute focused on the issue at Technical University of Munich.

Outside Silicon Valley, a company called Equivant created COMPAS, a machine-learning algorithm to predict whether current criminal defendants might commit future crimes, *Minority Report*-style. It didn't work quite as planned, though—it assumed more criminality from black defendants than white defendants, thanks in part to the data it was fed in the first place.

In response, a few tech companies have begun work on tools to help stop biased algorithms. Microsoft announced a still-unnamed product in May 2018 that aims to catch bias and stamp it out. Around the same time, Facebook launched its own product, called Fairness Flow, that would do the same thing, starting with the algorithm it uses to connect job seekers and employers on Facebook. The social-media giant created its bias-busting project with the help of a few other organizations, including the Center for Social Media Responsibility at the University of Michigan.

But details about how these programs will actually work are sparse, and they aren't being used yet. And to some experts, they seem like Band-Aids at best.

Cathy O'Neil, a mathematician and data-science writer, doesn't buy it at all.

I called O'Neil because I had read her book *Weapons of Math Destruction: How Big Data Increases Inequality and Threatens Democracy*, about all the ways algorithms can end up creating more problems than they solve and what can be done to prevent that. I had seen her speak on a panel about a year earlier and had been following her tech criticism on Twitter. I hoped she'd share some ideas for a better future, and maybe even some optimism. But shortly after our call began, I realized my memory had edited out one important thing about O'Neil: she is the opposite of sanguine about the tech industry. When I asked her about addressing the apparent unintended consequences of a homogenous group of people creating algorithms to run our social lives—consequences like racist AI and widespread trolling and harassment—she stopped me and proposed a thought experiment: What if the consequences weren't exactly unintended?

"We want to be careful about imputing motives, but you should have a spectrum of assumptions," she said. "One of them is that they wished it was easier to fix, but they didn't actually care about it enough or have enough time to work on it or whatever. The second possibility is that they didn't think about it at all, they just did the easiest possible thing that seemed to work. The third is that they wanted it to be hard."

In a *New York Times* review of two books by two of the fathers of VR, Jeremy Bailenson and Jaron Lanier, O'Neil pointed out what she says the books fail to: the obvious possibility that nefarious people might use their artful technologies not for empathy and compassion, but for pain and manipulation. One common expectation of both VR and AI is that it will be used for sex. In fact, it already is, by people who can afford a multithousand-dollar sex bot. O'Neil asked, in her review, "What would happen if abusive or pedophiliac makers got their hands on the controls?" And I think about the sex robot, Samantha, that was molested so much at a recent tech conference that it was severely damaged. Once technology becomes democratized, as is the stated goal for VR and AI, as with social networking and video-content creation, anyone can make anything they want. This raises questions about whether there should be limits, and if so, what they should be. It also leads a lot of skeptics to wonder why the people at the top don't seem to speak out about these issues more often.

"I think it's because [they] are themselves the current gatekeepers of this exciting technology, and although they plan for it to go mainstream, they desperately want it to be good for society," O'Neil wrote. "But Bailenson and Lanier cannot have it both ways: insisting that VR is very realistic, and thus affecting and potentially therapeutic, but also that it will be used only for good. That will happen only if it remains expensive and if the technology stalls. Fat chance."

For her part, O'Neil is all for empathy, but she doesn't expect change to come through appeals. She'd rather sue or attack the problem through academia. In 2017 she proposed the creation of an institute aimed at researching algorithmic bias and ways to prevent it in the future. An algorithmic accountability institute would, she wrote, provide ethical training for future engineers and data scientists, offer workshops to highlight the connections between AI and other industries (law, journalism, etc.) and create standards for "human experimentation in the age of big data."

Litigation and academia are long-term solutions. In the meantime, there are multiple other revolts from without and within.

From Digital Dependence to Digital Wellness

At the Wisdom 2.0 conference in San Francisco in 2018, moderator and conference founder Soren Gordhamer had come right out and asked Google's Empathy Lab director, Danielle Krettek, what it would look like if everyone had an empathetic phone. Krettek gave a roundabout answer that felt like part excuse, part commiseration:

> Ten years ago, when I was working on the iPhone, I had no idea that it would live in every nook and cranny of my experience, that it would be there when I was sad and when I was relieved and when I was happy, when I was with a bunch of people or by myself, first thing in the morning and last at night. Yet it's totally tone-deaf. On/off is a joke. "Do Not Disturb" is radically insufficient for the emotional gradient it is showing up for.

Phones have modes, but we have moods, she said, admitting that the tech industry thus far has not done a good job of acknowledging the full humanness of humans. The answer wasn't to make a phone more human, she seemed to say, but to make it more attentive to our experiences and how it shapes them. Tech's EQ needed to start matching its IQ, she argued.

Gordhamer told her it took a lot of courage to start an empathy lab at Google, which may or may not be true. It may be controversial among the largely homogenous tech industry to talk about feelings, but it's a good look brandwise as people and policymakers become increasingly concerned about privacy, data collection, and political influence. Krettek sees the current climate as a "challenging and beautiful opportunity" and also, it seems, as a do-over. "Designing for social interaction requires so much more of us to show up," she said. "Bringing all of who you are, all of yourself to the table, to the challenge, to the messy uncomfortable struggle of what it is to be human—you don't get to skip that this time. The next ten years are going to be very different."

The counterfactual O'Neil presented to me—that the creators of the tech we currently have, and struggle with, might have been either negligent, careless, or malicious—coupled with Krettek's comments, which I watched on YouTube a few days after she made them, together gave me another chance to turn my empathy on the tech founders themselves. If I really were Jeff Bezos or Mark Zuckerberg, if I had their demographics and backgrounds and experiences and privileges, I might not ever even think to worry about the impact AI could have on my résumé or rap sheet. I'd have concerns, sure, but they would be different. And if I hired mostly people with similar experiences and concerns, would I think twice about the echo chamber this created? (Especially if I were in the business of creating echo chambers, as some of these CEOs are?)

Much like what happened when I heard Dylan Marron's conversation with a commenter on *Conversations with People Who Hate Me*, this thought experiment didn't absolve these men in my eyes. It didn't release them from responsibility, but it released me from expecting something different. This made room in my mind for expecting better from the new pipeline of future-makers.

Brian Acton, cofounder of the messaging app WhatsApp, which he sold to Facebook for $19 billion, left $850 million on the table when he quit in 2018 (he took a screenshot of the stock price). He isn't anti-Facebook now, he told *Forbes*, he just got frustrated with their business-above-all-else strategy. Acton didn't want to advertise to WhatsApp users or track their data—he understood that these were two of the reasons people chose to use WhatsApp over other messaging services, including Facebook Messenger. But Facebook insisted, so Acton bailed and put some of his fortune toward Signal, an encrypted messaging app.

Others are taking less expensive but in some ways equally drastic action. In fall 2018, one of Instagram's original employees, Bailey

Richardson, told her twenty thousand followers that she was quitting the platform altogether. Like other social media, she said, it had become an unhealthy obsession for too many people rather than a friendly scrapbook. "In the early days," Richardson told the *Washington Post*, "you felt your post was seen by people who cared about you and that you cared about. That feeling is completely gone for me now." In late 2017, *Guardian* journalist Paul Lewis wrote about a growing number of Silicon Valley employees swearing off the very platforms they'd helped build, in part because they were afraid of what their products were doing to users' minds. "All of us are jacked into this system," Tristan Harris, a former Google employee, told Lewis. "All of our minds can be hijacked. Our choices are not as free as we think they are."

Harris is now a vocal critic of the industry and has dedicated much of the past several years to a nonprofit called the Center for Humane Technology, aimed at helping people use technology more intentionally and recognize warning signs of compulsive behavior and burnout. The organization encourages the developers of new and existing technology to have more empathy for their users, focusing on the quality of time spent with their products rather than the quantity. It also provides tips for users on how to take back control of their time from their smart-phones, with suggestions like turning off all notifications except those that come from actual people (i.e., texts) and switching the phone's screen to grayscale so as not to be drawn in by colorful and distracting apps.

Growing worries about how tech is affecting users have helped lead to an entirely new industry: digital wellness. Harris is one of its pioneers, not exactly shunning technology but prescribing healthier ways of using it and encouraging developers to have more empathy for their users.

Kunal Gupta may be Harris's Canadian counterpart. He is a tech entrepreneur, but he doesn't have email on his phone, he's not on social media, and he runs tech-free meetings at Polar, his digital-advertising firm. He doesn't even watch Netflix. He's currently working on creating a network, called the Mindtech Institute, to help tech entrepreneurs be more mindful and encourage them to invest in projects that aim to solve mental-health problems. I talked to Gupta over Google Hangouts on a day that I was feeling particularly frazzled by social media myself. After we'd been talking for a little while, I confessed to him that I had enlisted my husband to change my Facebook password and keep it from me at several points during the process of writing this book. I just couldn't stop opening the app and scrolling mindlessly when I got stuck or needed a distraction, and I would get caught up in some controversial post or news article and lose track of time.

"Please put that in the book," he half laughed. Then he promised to convince me to quit social media altogether.

He didn't seem completely serious about that last part, but social media is something that worries him. Through his own experience and access to research via his seat on the board of Canada's Centre for Addiction and Mental Health, he's become convinced that many of us currently use social media the way a lot of people smoked in the 1960s.

"Cigarettes were part of pretty much the whole twentieth century—part of advertisements, part of pop culture, everything," he said. "Then researchers figured out, oh, there's some health consequences to this."

The result was legislation, litigation, and a shift in advertising from pro-cigarette to anti-smoking, even on cigarette packaging itself. But it took eighty years to get there.

"I don't see how social media is any different," Gupta told me. "The research is starting to come out. I don't think it will take decades like it did for smoking."

Social media could potentially see a similar trajectory to cigarette smoking—the research is being funded (at least in Canada), we might have regulation (even Zuckerberg has admitted this might be the answer), and we certainly already have litigation, though clear precedent about the impact on users' mental health will be hard to come by.

Gupta said he sometimes feels like an outlier in the tech world for taking this view, but he believes the concern is spreading. When we talked, he had recently come back from a conference in San Francisco called Anxiety Tech. "It was fascinating to be in the Valley with a group of people who were talking about how technology is creating anxiety and depression in society," he said. "But also, how to take technology that's being used to help address different anxieties, and how within technology as an industry the culture at times is not one of empathy or compassion."

Apple, Google, and Facebook have all recently introduced so-called digital wellness features. The latest Apple operating system includes a screen-time tracker that shows not just how often you're using your phone, but what you're using it for. I have friends who have started to challenge themselves to get the number down—one averages about four hours per day, with the majority of that time spent on Instagram. My average is closer to two hours, depending on how much I'm craving distraction, and the vast majority of that is Instagram for me too. I know it isn't good for me to spend so much time watching other people's lives happen, but it is hard to resist the pull.

Luckily there are apps for that as well—from Moment, which tracks your usage and reminds you of daily limits, to Stay on Task, which will just pop up and ask if you are on task throughout the day, somewhat passive-aggressively reminding you to stay off social-networking and other apps and get to work.

The self-awareness inherent in these features, and that Gupta witnessed at the Anxiety Tech conference, is somehow both depressing and encouraging. But the psychology on the other side—of dopamine hits with every notification—remains powerful. The social-media companies wanted to change the world, and they certainly did. But the consequences have been more intense and varied than most at the helm could have imagined.

As new kinds of technology evolve, there's a new guard arguing that it's well past time we get better at imagining. Kamal Sinclair, a film producer at Sundance, is working on accomplishing just that.

The Changing Ethics of New Tech

In Making a New Reality, a research project funded by the Ford Foundation and published by digital-publishing platform Medium, Sinclair lays out the biggest gaps in equality and justice in current digital media, and makes a case for the requirement of diversity in emerging media like VR and AI. In one installment, she quoted producer Loira Limbal on the current fatal flaw of VR: "If people don't see communities that are typically thought of as 'other' as human, I don't think that a VR piece is going to humanize them." It's a false premise, Limbal argued, that relies on a trope of putting a "human face" on someone who is considered "other," i.e., not the cultural norm of white, male, straight, cis, and able-bodied.

Look no further than the controversial comments of Palmer Luckey, the founder of Oculus, which powers many of the virtual-reality experiences aimed at creating empathy. At a conference in 2014, he said that he felt it was his moral duty to bring VR to everyone, because "everyone wants to have a happy life . . . but it's going to be impossible to give everyone everything they want." So, his logic goes, people (such as "Chinese workers or people who are living in Africa") should have the opportunity to experience a "good" life through VR. This, many argued, was just the high-tech version of the "white savior" trope.

This innate limitation of VR—that its empathy impact depends largely on who's wearing the headset—is one problem. Its potential to cause actual harm is another, and that depends in large part on who's programming the content inside the headset. More often than not, that person fits the abovementioned cultural norm, but people like Sinclair,

Limbal, Courtney Cogburn, and filmmaker Michèle Stephenson are changing that.

I met Stephenson at a small café next to Prospect Park in Brooklyn. She has the look of someone who has lived in New York all her life—confident, assured, ready for anything, with springy curls and cautious eyes. A former human-rights attorney, Stephenson is now fully immersed in the documentary world. She and her partner became renowned in the independent-film world in 2013 for *American Promise*, a thirteen-year documentary they created, following their son and his best friend from kindergarten through graduation from the Dalton School. The way she sees it, empathy is key to a documentary—"It's a given, otherwise your story's no good," she said.

Stephenson tells stories about the systemic issues and barriers to success for communities of color. She makes films, gives talks, writes books, and has made apps to help parents and educators of children of color. A couple of years ago she embarked on her first virtual-reality project, about racial violence and discrimination and their connection to the long legacy of slavery and white supremacy, called *The Changing Same: The Racial Justice Project*. Stephenson calls it magical-realist time travel—it takes the user on a journey with the ghost of a 1934 lynching victim named Claude Neal, from the time of his ancestors, to his horrific death, to a visit with his descendants in the present day. It's a harrowing reminder of our country's history and how little things have changed, but it's also about hope, with reminders of different possibilities, sprinkled with hints of Afrofuturism. That's what it felt like to talk with Stephenson too.

For much of the tech and new-media industries, she told me over lunch, it seems a given that viewers will relate to a largely white and male experience. Who is telling the story will always affect which stories get told and how they are portrayed. Slavery and mass incarceration are everyone's collective history and present, not just those of black Americans, Stephenson reminds me, and we won't get past our divisions until we all recognize this. *The Changing Same* is meant to help start this conversation, but it has a deeper purpose as well. It isn't just for nonblack people who need to understand the deepness of racial inequity in America; it's a way to address the inequity itself.

"Especially in the emerging media space, we cannot allow the dominant culture to tell how our stories will unfold, or how they can be told, and who the audience is that we're appealing to," she said. "We're putting a stake in the ground."

That effort includes creating a variety of VR experiences aimed at a different audience than most: young black people who are looking for ways to gain a better understanding of history, and to heal. She sees her job as helping democratize access to this medium. But as a storyteller, she said, "if we do our job well, hopefully everybody's going to want to go through our ritual."

In talking to tech CEOs and entrepreneurs, I was looking not necessarily for solutions, but for solutions-oriented people and projects. I wanted to know whether other people had the same concerns I had, and more importantly, whether any of those people were in a position to do anything about it. Over the two years I spent researching and conducting interviews, I realized that the answer to the first question is a resounding yes, and the answer to the second question is probably "Not yet."

But throughout the process I also realized that at times I was asking the wrong questions. When looking toward a future in which empathy and technology are intimately intertwined—for good, and not for manipulation—it would be naive to ignore the major players, but it would be even worse to assume they will do what's right. Those of us outside the industry with questions about it, and the young people we raise and teach, might be the best equipped to prepare us for, and propel us toward, a more empathic future.

It can also be too easy to place blame on the companies that helped us get to where we are now, for better or worse. In some cases, it's true—they don't care. In others, they simply didn't—and may still not—know any better. Some are making real efforts to inject empathy into their existing and upcoming products and services. It can be hard to tell which is which, and the more I've spoken to and read the work of emerging leaders like Kamal Sinclair, Cathy O'Neil, Michèle Stephenson, Ami Shah, Kunal Gupta, and Robyn Janz—to name just a few—the less I feel the need to focus on the Silicon Valley giants. These other creators, thinkers, and activists might be called the builders of the second wave of the tech revolution. They are more diverse, more skeptical, more transparent, and, yes, more empathetic, in their work and their communications. My conversations with these people gave me hope that we really will have a feeling future.

Even amid these new thinkers, not everyone agrees on what this future should look like. But the difference from the last time around seems to be that everything is on the table—and more than just a handful of people are sitting around it. Ultimately their goal isn't to outsource our emotions to technology, or to make technology more human. It's to make *us* more human, with the help of the tools we've created without fully knowing how to use them. They want to teach us how to learn from our mistakes, but also how to be prepared to solve the future problems we, humans that we are, will create for ourselves.

EPILOGUE
WHAT'S NEXT

Many of these technologies already exist in some form. Virtual reality has been available in various incarnations for decades, as has AI. Chatbots are in full use by many companies for when you'd rather not call a human for customer service. All of this has become normalized in our lives relatively quickly, but the experts I spoke with regularly reminded me that we haven't seen anything yet. Among other things, they taught me that much of what we have learned to see as science fiction is not just possible—it's already a reality.

"Technologies that allow us to track and sense emotions and share or broadcast them with others are going through a huge explosion of development and breakthrough research right now," said Jane McGonigal, director of game research and development at the Institute for the Future, who helped create the Face the Future game. She came up with the FeelThat, the fictional headset that the young girl in the game's introduction video wore to transmit her feelings to others and receive theirs. "It may seem like a leap to think people will want to be broadcasting their innermost feelings, but if we think about it, ten years ago, the idea that we would be sharing our location and photos of intimate moments with the world like we do on Instagram and

Foursquare seemed like a leap. There seems to be no limit to people's appetite to share."

She pointed me to the Thync, a triangular device created by neuroscientists at the Massachusetts Institute of Technology that is, according to marketing materials, "the first consumer health solution for lowering stress and anxiety." The device electrically stimulates the nerves in the user's face and neck that have been found to help regulate stress hormones. It's touted as the lower-tech, lower-risk version of brain stimulation, and some research shows it can help treat epilepsy, anxiety, and depression.

This is not exactly the FeelThat, but the ability to change someone's state of mind with a few vibrations could be one step in that direction. McGonigal and many of her colleagues believe that within a decade, "there may be other ways to simulate the feelings other people are feeling" originating from these initial findings. And Thync isn't alone. In January 2016, Apple purchased Emotient, an artificial-intelligence company that has developed facial-recognition software that detects, and tags, people's emotions. Digital assistants like Siri and Amazon's Alexa have the ability to detect mental states through voice patterns. Wearables like the Fitbit can already track your heart rate and potentially identify arrhythmias; soon enough, they could have sweat sensors to detect hormones like adrenaline, cortisol, and oxytocin, which tend to spike when we are excited, stressed, or anxious. A single device with the ability to do all of these things wouldn't be far off from the still-fictional FeelThat, unboxed by the young girl with the big smile.

At times I have wished for a tool like the FeelThat. Would contentious Facebook conversations have been more bearable—and maybe even productive—if I could have literally shared my feelings with the other person, and vice versa? But it's hard not to think about what the next step might be. As the kids who participated in the Face the Future game worried: What if the tech that allowed us to share our feelings could also manipulate it? We've already seen this kind of manipulation with the proliferation of trolls and bots feeding us false stories and photos (and now even videos) on social media. Would I really want to be able to share my feelings with someone who could use them against me—literally or figuratively?

But some people are ready to go even further. When I asked her what she hopes for the future of empathic technology, Bulbul Gupta, of Socos Labs, said: "In my dream I have literally a little chip in my brain that can send my thoughts, translated by text or email or whatever way I think them, because then maybe that would help me be the fully efficient human being I want to be. I could keep track of all kinds of different stuff without a ton of different apps." To her, empathic tech isn't about the technology itself showing empathy, or encouraging her to be more empathetic; it's about the creators of the tech having empathy for the end user—in this case, a super busy woman with a career in tech, a child, and a very digital-focused life.

Vivienne Ming, founder of Socos and creator of the Muse app, pointed me to neural dust: tiny wireless sensors being developed at the University of California, Berkeley that could be used to noninvasively monitor vitals and other things going on in the body. Ming herself is currently working with a startup creating noninvasive technology to expand working memory. According to Ming, there are only two places to get funding for something like that right now—DARPA (the Defense Advanced Research Projects Agency) and the professional computer-gaming industry.

"Right now, it's essentially funding steroids for computer gamers," she said. "I'm helping them build up the technology and advising them in exchange for being able to use it for kids with traumatic brain injuries."

Eugenia Kuyda, creator of the Replika bot that made me happier than my Talkspace therapist, is still dreaming of true conversational AI. "I have a huge belief that maybe in three, four, five years we'll see conversations where we can create an emotional connection with a bot, and help people have great conversations that make them feel better," she said. "The dream will be the same in five years as it is now: to see a machine talk to a human being and make this human happier."

Gupta, of Socos Labs, said, "When I think of what the future looks like, I think about all of these amazing technologies that we can create. How do we ensure that they are used ethically, designed ethically, and how do we work to mitigate for that? To make sure that we're setting up the right nudges, the right sort of principles and guidelines, and frameworks that are light-touch enough for entrepreneurs to actually use, but [are] ethical enough and [have] safeguards enough for building the more inclusive future that we want and not just increasing the vast sort of deficit between the haves and the have-nots."

At the beginning of this journey, I regularly found myself losing hours to Facebook with nothing to show for it but a headache; I also tended to use Twitter and Instagram as crutches for boredom and anxiety, opening the apps almost instinctively whenever I had a free moment or an uncomfortable thought. I'd be lying if I said I've completely broken these habits, but I have made some changes.

The biggest move I made was to deactivate Facebook. This is probably a temporary change until I can figure out a healthier relationship with the platform, one in which empathy plays a larger role than the dopamine rush. Toward that end, I've also stopped reading comments on news articles and mostly stopped reading them on Instagram posts. I still get bogged down in Twitter threads sometimes, but that's one area where I've started to follow more people who are different from me, and I spend most of my time there reading instead of posting.

When it comes to adopting new technology, I've put together a personal checklist based in part on advice from the people I've interviewed and in part on my own intuition. When I hear about a new app, gadget, or tech-based service, I try to ask myself the following questions:

- How might this improve my life or experience, or those of others?
- What is the potential for it to be manipulated, and are there safeguards? Is there incentive for the people in charge to monitor this—do they have skin in the game? And ultimately, do I think the rewards will outweigh the risks?
- Are terms, practices, and concerns transparent and open to critique by users?
- Does this technology, or do its founders and funders, have a reputation for intentionally or inadvertently harming and marginalizing others? Are they actively working to change/avoid that?

Those are the parameters I have decided are most important to me right now as I consider my own relationship to technology, as well as in a not-too-distant future in which my niece and nephews—and eventually, maybe, my own children—interact daily with tools and bots I can't even imagine yet. Your questions might be different, and they will likely evolve as time goes on. But we should continue to ask them, because barring something cataclysmic, our future will likely be even more tech focused than the present. We can't control all the tech products that come at us, but we should assert some agency in how they affect our lives.

ACKNOWLEDGMENTS

I don't know if I would have gone through with this if Meredith Talusan hadn't welcomed me into a small writing group at her apartment in New York in 2017. To Meredith, Lilly, Tim, Nina, Kaye, Lewis, and Voichita: thank you for pushing me, questioning me, encouraging me, brainstorming with me, and teaching me how to see myself as a writer deserving of all that, and all this.

While my friends and colleagues gave me guidance and courage, this book wouldn't exist without the many people who agreed to be interviewed, shadowed, and emailed over and over. The people in this book are doing hard, change-making work, and I want to express my gratitude for their willingness to share it.

To Dr. Tony Lamair Burks II, thank you for seeing the light in me as an anxious teenager and continuing to remind me it's there during my darkest times. Thank you for teaching me the historical, cultural, and spiritual importance of storytelling, and showing me its worth as a vocation and an art form.

For teaching me the basics and challenging me to do more, my thanks to Drs. Heather Coffey, Anthony Hatcher, and David Copeland. For editing me to within an inch of my life, thank you Jocelyn Allison and Michael Peltz—those experiences pushed me to report the hell out of this book. For giving the ideas and words in this book their first breaths in the world outside my laptop, thank you Lilly Dancyger and Brendan Spiegel at Narratively and Nikki Gloudeman at the Establishment. I'm so grateful to every friend who read a chapter and listened to me talk about this book incessantly; my agent, Jill Marsal, for seeing the potential in my proposal and advocating for me; and my editor, Erin Calligan Mooney at Little A, for nurturing the story with me.

Thanks, Mom and Dad, for supporting my ideas and aspirations even when you didn't understand them. Thank you, Grandma, for helping me open my mind and feeding me while I edited furiously on your porch. Thank you, Anya, for keeping me laughing, and Michele, Seth, and Marissa, for the endless baby photos that cheered me up on tough days. Thank you, Angela and Steve, for letting me use your house as a writing retreat, and for all the wine.

And thank you, Reid, for sitting with me at Abilene and listening to me speak this idea out loud for the first time over Dark 'N Stormys. Thank you for not just saying yes, but being as excited about it as I was. Thank you for the patience, the coffee and sandwiches, the reminders of how far I'd come every time I felt stuck, letting me mope when it was "part of the process," and never letting me give up. I love you.

BIBLIOGRAPHY

6×9. (Virtual-reality video.) *Guardian*, April 27, 2016. https://www.theguardian.com/world/ng-interactive/2016/apr/27/6x9-a-virtual-experience-of-solitary-confinement.

Abedon, Emily Perlman. "Toddler Empathy." *Parents* magazine website, accessed May 22, 2019. https://www.parents.com/toddlers-preschoolers/development/behavioral/toddler-empathy.

Anderson, Melinda D. "How Internet Filtering Hurts Kids." *Atlantic*, April 26, 2016. https://www.theatlantic.com/education/archive/2016/04/internet-filtering-hurts-kids/479907.

Archer, Dan, and Katharina Finger. "Walking in Another's Virtual Shoes: Do 360-Degree Video News Stories Generate Empathy in Viewers?" Tow Center for Digital Journalism, *Columbia Journalism Review*, March 15, 2018. https://www.cjr.org/tow_center_reports/virtual-reality-news-empathy.php.

Attwood, Angela S., Kayleigh E. Easey, Michael N. Dalili, Andrew L. Skinner, Andy Woods, Lana Crick, Elizabeth Ilett, Ian S. Penton-Voak, and Marcus R. Munafò. "State Anxiety and Emotional Face Recognition in Healthy Volunteers." *Royal Society Open Science*

4, no. 5 (May 1, 2017). https://royalsocietypublishing.org/doi/full/10.1098/rsos.160855.

Barlow, Rich. "Is Your Computer Sexist?" BU Today, December 6, 2016. http://www.bu.edu/today/2016/sexist-computer.

Bartneck, Christoph, and Jun Hu. "Exploring the Abuse of Robots." *Interaction Studies—Social Behaviour and Communication in Biological and Artificial Systems* 9, no. 3 (2008): 415–33. http://www.bartneck.de/publications/2008/exploreAbuseRobots.

Batson, C. Daniel, Johee Chang, Ryan Orr, and Jennifer Rowland. "Empathy, Attitudes, and Action: Can Feeling for a Member of a Stigmatized Group Motivate One to Help the Group?" *Personality and Social Psychology Bulletin* 28, no. 12 (December 2002): 1656–66. https://journals.sagepub.com/doi/abs/10.1177/014616702237647.

Bernardo, Monica Oliveira, Dario Cecílio-Fernandes, Patrício Costa, Thelma A. Quince, Manuel João Costa, and Marco Antonio Carvalho-Filho. "Physicians' Self-Assessed Empathy Levels Do Not Correlate with Patients' Assessments." *PLOS ONE* 13, no. 5 (May 31, 2018). https://www.ncbi.nlm.nih.gov/pubmed/29852021.

Berryman, Chloe, Christopher J. Ferguson, Charles Negy. "Social Media Use and Mental Health among Young Adults." *Psychiatric Quarterly* 89, no. 2 (June 2018): 307–14. http://christopherjferguson.com/Vaguebooking.pdf.

Bhutani, Jaikrit, Sukriti Bhutani, Yatan Pal Balhara, and Sanjay Kalra. "Compassion Fatigue and Burnout Amongst Clinicians: A Medical Exploratory Study." *Indian Journal of Psychological Medicine* 34, no.

4 (October 2012): 332–37. https://www.ncbi.nlm.nih.gov/pmc/articles/PMC3662129.

Bogle, Ariel. "Artificial Intelligence Is Being Trained to Have Empathy. Should We Be Worried?" Australian Broadcasting Corporation, June 1, 2018. https://www.abc.net.au/news/science/2018-06-02/can-you-trust-a-robot-that-cares/9808636.

Brandt, Galen. "Crossing the Threshold: A 'Detour' into Healing." VirtualGalen.com (the website of Galen Brandt), accessed May 22, 2019. http://www.virtualgalen.com/virtualhealing/braininjury.htm.

Brockwell, Holly. "Forgotten Genius: The Man Who Made a Working VR Machine in 1957." TechRadar, April 3, 2016. https.//www.techradar.com/news/wearables/forgotten-genius-the-man-who-made-a-working-vr-machine-in-1957-1318253.

Brooker, Charlie. "The Dark Side of Our Gadget Addiction." *Guardian*, December 1, 2011. https://www.theguardian.com/technology/2011/dec/01/charlie-brooker-dark-side-gadget-addiction-black-mirror.

Brown, Ariella. "AR for Empathy: The Devastation of War." DMN, April 3, 2018. https://www.dmnews.com/customer-experience/article/13034609/ar-for-empathy-the-devastation-of-war.

Bury, Liz. "Reading Literary Fiction Improves Empathy, Study Finds." *Guardian*, October 8, 2013. https://www.theguardian.com/books/booksblog/2013/oct/08/literary-fiction-improves-empathy-study.

Cadwalladr, Carole, and Emma Graham-Harrison. "Revealed: 50 Million Facebook Profiles Harvested for Cambridge Analytica in Major Data Breach." *Guardian*, March 17, 2018. https://www.theguardian.com/news/2018/mar/17/cambridge-analytica-facebook-influence-us-election.

Cameron, C. D., and B. K. Payne. "Escaping Affect: How Motivated Emotion Regulation Creates Insensitivity to Mass Suffering." *Journal of Personality and Social Psychology* 100, no. 1 (2011): 1–15. http://dx.doi.org/10.1037/a0021643.

Center for Humane Technology. Website accessed May 22, 2019. https://humanetech.com.

Chung, Caleb. "Come Play with Pleo the Dinosaur." TED Talk video, December 2, 2008. https://www.youtube.com/watch?v=mGZzx8OdHWo.

Cornell Computing and Information Science. "Cornell Researchers Predict When Online Conversations Turn Toxic." Cornell University website, accessed May 22, 2019. https://cis.cornell.edu/cornell-researchers-predict-when-online-conversations-turn-toxic.

Dastin, Jeffrey. "Amazon Scraps Secret AI Recruiting Tool That Showed Bias against Women." Reuters, October 9, 2018. https://www.reuters.com/article/us-amazon-com-jobs-automation-insight/amazon-scraps-secret-ai-recruiting-tool-that-showed-bias-against-women-idUSKCN1MK08G.

Davis, Ben. "Can VR Really Make Us Feel Empathy? Alejandro G. Iñárritu's 'Carne y Arena' Proves That's the Wrong Question." Artnet News, March 30, 2018. https://news.artnet.com/exhibitions/alejandro-g-inarritus-carne-y-arena-comes-to-dc-1255907.

De Witte, Melissa. "A New Report by Stanford Researchers and Common Sense Media Examines the Potential Effect of Virtual Reality on Children." Stanford News, April 4, 2018. https://news.stanford.edu/2018/04/04/emerging-research-shows-potential-power-vr-kids.

Dholakia, Utpal. "How Long Does Public Empathy Last After a Natural Disaster?" *Psychology Today*, September 24, 2017. https://www.psychologytoday.com/us/blog/the-science-behind-behavior/201709/how-long-does-public-empathy-last-after-natural-disaster.

Dwoskin, Elizabeth, Michael Alison Chandler, and Brian Fung. "Auschwitz, Sex Assault and Police Shootings—Where Virtual Reality Is Going Next." *The Washington Post*, November 11, 2016. https://www.washingtonpost.com/news/the-switch/wp/2016/11/11/auschwitz-sex-assault-and-police-shootings-where-virtual-reality-is-going-next.

Dwoskin, Elizabeth. "Quitting Instagram: She's One of the Millions Disillusioned with Social Media. But She also Helped Create It." *Washington Post*, November 13, 2018. https://www.washingtonpost.com/technology/2018/11/14/quitting-instagram-shes-one-millions-disillusioned-with-social-media-she-also-helped-create-it.

Ehmke, Rachel. "How Using Social Media Affects Teenagers." Child Mind Institute, accessed May 22, 2019. https://childmind.org/article/how-using-social-media-affects-teenagers.

Ehmke, Rachel. "How Using Social Media Affects Teenagers." Website of Child Mind Institute, accessed May 22, 2019. https://childmind.org/article/how-using-social-media-affects-teenagers.

Emerson, Joelle. "Don't Give Up on Unconscious Bias Training— Make It Better." *Harvard Business Review*, April 28, 2017. https://hbr.org/2017/04/dont-give-up-on-unconscious-bias-training-make-it-better.

Epstude, Kai, and Neal J. Roese. "The Functional Theory of Counterfactual Thinking." *Personality and Social Psychology Review* 12, no. 2: 168–92. https://www.ncbi.nlm.nih.gov/pmc/articles/PMC2408534.

Facing History School. Homepage, accessed May 22, 2019. http://www.facinghistoryschool.org.

Fanselow, Erika E. "Central Mechanisms of Cranial Nerve Stimulation for Epilepsy." *Surgical Neurology International* 3, suppl. 4 (October 31, 2012): S247–54. https://www.ncbi.nlm.nih.gov/pmc/articles/PMC3514917.

Feldblum, Chai R., and Victoria A. Lipnic. *Select Task Force on the Study of Harassment in the Workplace.* US Equal Employment Opportunity Commission, June 2016. https://www.eeoc.gov/eeoc/task_force/harassment/report.cfm.

Frenkel, Sheera, Nicholas Confessore, Cecilia Kang, Matthew Rosenberg, and Jack Nicas. "Delay, Deny and Deflect: How Facebook's Leaders Fought Through Crisis." *New York Times*, November 14, 2018. https://www.nytimes.com/2018/11/14/technology/facebook-data-russia-election-racism.html.

Fussell, Sidney. "Pearson Embedded a 'Social-Psychological' Experiment in Students' Educational Software." Gizmodo,

April 18, 2018. https://gizmodo.com/pearson-embedded-a-social-psychological-experiment-in-s-1825367784.

Galluzzo, Gary. "How Do Toddlers Use Tablets?" Iowa Now, website of the University of Iowa, June 18, 2015. https://now.uiowa.edu/2015/06/how-do-toddlers-use-tablets.

Gao, Wei, Sam Emaminejad, Hnin Yin Yin Nyein, Samyuktha Challa, Kevin Chen, Austin Peck, Hossain M. Fahad, Hiroki Ota, Hiroshi Shiraki, Daisuke Kiriya, Der-Hsien Lien, George A. Brooks, Ronald W. Davis, and Ali Javey. "Fully Integrated Wearable Sensor Arrays for Multiplexed In Situ Perspiration Analysis." *Nature* 529 (28 January 2016): 509–14. https://www.nature.com/articles/nature16521.epdf.

Garvie, Clare, Alvaro Bedoya, and Jonathan Frankle. *The Perpetual Line-Up: Unregulated Police Face Recognition in America.* Report published by Georgetown Law Center on Privacy & Technology, October 18, 2016. https://www.perpetuallineup.org.

Gerace, Adam. "Does Past Experience Increase Empathy?" *Psychology Today*, August 24, 2017. https://www.psychologytoday.com/us/blog/knowing-me-knowing-you/201708/does-past-experience-increase-empathy.

Gibbs, Samuel. "Apple's Tim Cook: 'I Don't Want My Nephew on a Social Network.'" *Guardian*, January 19, 2018. https://www.theguardian.com/technology/2018/jan/19/tim-cook-i-dont-want-my-nephew-on-a-social-network.

Google News Lab. "STORYLIVING: An Ethnographic Study of How Audiences Experience VR and What That Means for Journalists."

Google News Initiative, July 28, 2017. https://newslab.withgoogle.
com/assets/docs/storyliving-a-study-of-vr-in-journalism.pdf.

Green, Melanie. "Why Is It So Stressful to Talk Politics with the Other
Side?" The Graduate School, University at Buffalo, April 11, 2018.
https://grad.buffalo.edu/news.host.html/content/shared/univer-
sity/news/ub-reporter-articles/stories/2018/04/green-talking-poli-
tics.detail.html.

Hardesty, Larry. "Study Finds Gender and Skin-Type Bias in
Commercial Artificial-Intelligence Systems." MIT News, February
11, 2018. http://news.mit.edu/2018/study-finds-gender-skin-
type-bias-artificial-intelligence-systems-0212.

Hart-Davidson, William, and Ryan Kilcoyne. "Web App Facilitates
Better Online Conversations." Research@MSU, website of
Michigan State University, September 26, 2016. https://research.
msu.edu/web-app-facilitates-better-online-conversations.

Haynes, Trevor. "Dopamine, Smartphones & You: A Battle for Your
Time." Science in the News, the Graduate School of Arts and
Sciences, Harvard University, May 1, 2018. http://sitn.hms.har-
vard.edu/flash/2018/dopamine-smartphones-battle-time.

Healthy Child Manitoba. "Roots of Empathy." Website of the government of Manitoba, Canada, accessed May 22, 2019. https://www.
gov.mb.ca/healthychild/roe/index.html.

Hern, Alex. "'Never Get High On Your Own Supply'—Why Social
Media Bosses Don't Use Social Media." Guardian, January
23, 2018. https://www.theguardian.com/media/2018/jan/23/

never-get-high-on-your-own-supply-why-social-media-bosses-dont-use-social-media.

Herrema, Martin. "'Phubbing' Can Threaten Our Basic Human Needs." University of Kent, March 27, 2018. https://www.kent.ac.uk/news/society/17584/phubbing-can-threaten-our-basic-human-needs-research-shows.

Hojat, Mohammadreza, Michael J. Vergare, Kaye Maxwell, George Brainard, Steven K. Herrine, Gerald A. Isenberg, Jon Veloski, and Joseph S. Gonnella. "The Devil Is in the Third Year: A Longitudinal Study of Erosion of Empathy in Medical School." *Academic Medicine* 84, no. 9 (September 2009): 1182–91. https://www.ncbi.nlm.nih.gov/pubmed/19707055.

HOLO-DOODLE (website). Accessed May 22, 2019. http://www.holodoodle.net.

Horstmann, Aike C., Nikolai Bock, Eva Linhuber, Jessica M. Szczuka, Carolin Straßmann, and Nicole C. Krämer. "Do a Robot's Social Skills and Its Objection Discourage Interactants from Switching the Robot Off?" *PLOS ONE* 13, no. 7 (July 31, 2018). https://doi.org/10.1371/journal.pone.0201581.

Hutchinson Andrew. "YouTube Updates Recommendations Algorithm to Lessen the Spread of 'Borderline Content.'" Social Media Today, January 26, 2019. https://www.socialmediatoday.com/news/youtube-updates-recommendations-algorithm-to-lessen-the-spread-of-borderli/546906.

I Am Robot (website). Accessed May 22, 2019. http://www.iamrobot.fyi.

Institute for the Future. "Face the Future: A Game about the Future of Empathy." Website of Institute for the Future, accessed May 22, 2019. http://www.iftf.org/facethefuture.

Jaroszewski, Adam C., Robert R. Morris, and Matthew K. Nock. "Randomized Controlled Trial of an Online Machine Learning-Driven Risk Assessment and Intervention Platform for Increasing the Use of Crisis Services." *Journal of Consulting and Clinical Psychology* 87, no. 4 (2019): 370–79.

Jerabek, Ilona. "The Multiplicity of Empathy: Study Reveals Both Interpersonal & Intrapersonal Benefits of Being Empathetic." PRWeb, March 31, 2018. http://www.prweb.com/releases/2018/03/prweb15372302.htm.

Johnson, Sydney. "This Company Wants to Gather Student Brainwave Data to Measure 'Engagement.'" EdSurge, October 26, 2017. https://www.edsurge.com/news/2017-10-26-this-company-wants-to-gather-student-brainwave-data-to-measure-engagement.

Kahn, Peter H., Jr., Hiroshi Ishiguro, Brian T. Gill, Takayuki Kanda, Nathan G. Freier, Rachel L. Severson, Jolina H. Ruckert, and Solace Shen. "'Robovie, You'll Have to Go into the Closet Now': Children's Social and Moral Relationships with a Humanoid Robot." *Developmental Psychology* 48, no. 2 (2012): 303–14. https://depts.washington.edu/hints/publications/Robovie_Closet_Study_Developmental_Psych_2012.pdf.

Kang, Inkoo. "Oculus Whiffed." Slate, November 21, 2017. https://slate.com/technology/2017/11/virtual-reality-is-failing-at-empathy-its-biggest-promise.html.

Kellmeyer, Philipp, Oliver Mueller, Ronit Feingold-Polak, and Shelly Levy-Tzedek. "Social Robots in Rehabilitation: A Question of Trust." *Science Robotics* 3, no. 21 (August 15, 2018). https://robotics.sciencemag.org/content/3/21/eaat1587.

Kemp, Mike, and Richard S. Wellins. "The Economics of Empathy." *GO Magazine*, 2017 issue 1. https://www.ddiworld.com/go/archive/go-magazine-2017-issue-1/the-economics-of-empathy.

Kinsella, Ben G., Stephanie Chow, and Azadeh Kushki. "Evaluating the Usability of a Wearable Social Skills Training Technology for Children with Autism Spectrum Disorder." *Frontiers in Robotics and AI* 4, no. 31. https://www.frontiersin.org/articles/10.3389/frobt.2017.00031/full.

Klamer, Tineke, and Somaya Ben Allouch. "Acceptance and Use of a Social Robot by Elderly Users in a Domestic Environment." *2010 4th International Conference on Pervasive Computing Technologies for Healthcare*, Munich, 2010. https://eudl.eu/doi/10.4108/icst.pervasivehealth2010.8892.

Klick. "Sympulse PD—Jim and Pat." YouTube video, May 14, 2018. https://www.youtube.com/watch?v=Iu0sEGMDeBg.

Kolata, Gina. "Why Do Obese Patients Get Worse Care? Many Doctors Don't See Past the Fat." *New York Times*, September 25, 2016. https://www.nytimes.com/2016/09/26/health/obese-patients-health-care.html.

Konrath, Sara. "Americans Are More Socially Isolated, but Less Lonely." *Psychology Today*, May 7, 2018. https://www.

psychologytoday.com/us/blog/the-empathy-gap/201805/
americans-are-more-socially-isolated-less-lonely.

Kool, Hollis. "The Ethics of Immersive Journalism: A Rhetorical
Analysis of News Storytelling with Virtual Reality Technology."
Intersect: The Stanford Journal of Science, Technology, and Society 9,
no. 3 (June 2016): 1–11. http://ojs.stanford.edu/ojs/index.php/
intersect/article/view/871.

Kraus, Michael W. "Voice-Only Communication Enhances Empathic
Accuracy." *American Psychologist* 72, no. 7 (2017): 644–54. https://
www.apa.org/pubs/journals/releases/amp-amp0000147.pdf.

Kunzmann, Kevin. "Empathy from Physicians More Likely to Result
in Patient Information from Family." MD Magazine (website), July
9, 2018. https://www.mdmag.com/medical-news/empathy-from-
physicians-more-likely-to-result-in-patient-information-from-
family.

Lewis, Paul. "'Our Minds Can Be Hijacked': The Tech Insiders
Who Fear a Smartphone Dystopia." *Guardian*, October 6,
2017. https://www.theguardian.com/technology/2017/oct/05/
smartphone-addiction-silicon-valley-dystopia.

Ligman, Kris. You Are Jeff Bezos (web-based game). Accessed May 22,
2019. https://direkris.itch.io/you-are-jeff-bezos.

Lucas, Brian J., and Nour S. Kteily. "(Anti-)Egalitarianism
Differentially Predicts Empathy for Members of Advantaged
Versus Disadvantaged Groups." *Journal of Personality and Social
Psychology* 114, no. 5 (2018): 665–692. https://psycnet.apa.org/
record/2018-16714-002.

Lucas, Gale M., Albert Rizzo, Jonathan Gratch, Stefan Scherer, Giota Stratou, Jill Boberg, and Louis-Philippe Morency. "Reporting Mental Health Symptoms: Breaking Down Barriers to Care with Virtual Human Interviewers." *Frontiers in Robotics and AI* 4, no. 51 (October 2017). https://www.frontiersin.org/articles/10.3389/frobt.2017.00051/full.

Lucas, Gale M., Jonathan Gratch, Aisha King, and Louis-Philippe Morency. "It's Only a Computer: Virtual Humans Increase Willingness to Disclose." *Computers in Human Behavior* 37 (August 2014): 94–100. https://www.sciencedirect.com/science/article/pii/S0747563214002647.

Manyika, James, Susan Lund, Michael Chui, Jacques Bughin, Jonathan Woetzel, Parul Batra, Ryan Ko, and Saurabh Sanghvi. *Jobs Lost, Jobs Gained: What the Future of Work Will Mean for Jobs, Skills, and Wages.* McKinsey Global Institute, November 2017. https://www.mckinsey.com/featured-insights/future-of-work/jobs-lost-jobs-gained-what-the-future-of-work-will-mean-for-jobs-skills-and-wages.

Marinova, Polina. "The One Skill Employees Need to Survive the AI Revolution." *Fortune*, December 8, 2017. http://fortune.com/2017/12/07/machines-humans-jobs.

MarketWatch. "Healthcare/Medical Simulation Market Size Is Projected to Be Around US$2.50 Billion by 2022." Press release, August 17, 2018. https://www.marketwatch.com/press-release/healthcaremedical-simulation-market-size-is-projected-to-be-around-us-250-billion-by-2022-2018-08-17.

Marron, Dylan. "Every Single Word." Tumblr, last updated September 30, 2016. https://everysinglewordspoken.tumblr.com.

Marron, Dylan. "Trans Icon, Author & Activist KATE BORNSTEIN (Ep. 4)." *Sitting in Bathrooms with Trans People.* YouTube video (part of a series), October 20, 2016. https://www.youtube.com/watch?v=haYP5uA4Rsk.

Marron, Dylan. "Unboxing Masculinity." *Unboxing with Dylan Marron.* YouTube video (part of a series), September 20, 2016. https://www.youtube.com/watch?v=rHOjDZP2SWY.

Martinez, Mariela. "Floreo Awarded $1.7M NIH Grant to Test Whether VR Can Improve Police Safety in Individuals with ASD." Press release. Floreo, October 31, 2017. https://floreotech.com/2017/10/31/floreo-awarded-1-7m-nih-grant-to-test-whether-vr-can-improve-police-safety-in-individuals-with-asd.

Medina, John. "Is Technology Bad for the Teenage Brain? (Yes, No and It's Complicated.)." EdSurge, April 3, 2018. https://www.edsurge.com/news/2018-04-03-is-technology-bad-for-the-teenage-brain-yes-no-and-it-s-complicated.

Melnick, Kyle. "CEOs Under Fire for Using VR to Experience Being Homeless." VRScout, June 28, 2017. https://vrscout.com/news/ceos-vr-experience-homeless.

Mercer, Stewart W., Maria Higgins, Annemieke M. Bikker, Bridie Fitzpatrick, Alex McConnachie, Suzanne M. Lloyd, Paul Little, and Graham C. M. Watt. "General Practitioners' Empathy and Health Outcomes: A Prospective Observational Study of Consultations in Areas of High and Low Deprivation." *Annals of Family Medicine*

14, no. 2 (March/April 2016): 117–24. https://www.ncbi.nlm.nih. gov/pmc/articles/PMC4781514.

Merler, Michele, Nalini Ratha, Rogerio S. Feris, and John R. Smith. Diversity in Faces Dataset. IBM AI Research, accessed May 22, 2019. https://www.research.ibm.com/artificial-intelligence/ trusted-ai/diversity-in-faces.

Meyer, David. "Amazon Reportedly Killed an AI Recruitment System Because It Couldn't Stop the Tool from Discriminating Against Women." *Fortune*, October 10, 2018. http://fortune. com/2018/10/10/amazon-ai-recruitment-bias-women-sexist.

Michigan News. "Empathy: College Students Don't Have As Much As They Used To." University of Michigan, May 27, 2010. https://news.umich.edu/empathy-college-students-don-t-have- as-much-as-they-used-to.

Milk, Chris. "How Virtual Reality Can Create the Ultimate Empathy Machine." TED Talk video, March 2015. https://www.ted.com/ talks/chris_milk_how_virtual_reality_can_create_the_ultimate_ empathy_machine.

Moore, Pam. "Schools Are Teaching Kids Empathy and Self- Control. It Helps at Home, Too." *Northwest Herald*, February 22, 2018. https://www.nwherald.com/2018/02/22/schools-are- teaching-kids-empathy-and-self-control-it-helps-at-home-too/ ayyp0ck.

Moreno, Megan A. "Developer Discusses How App Builds Empathy, Research behind It." Random App of Kindness blog, August 16, 2017. http://www.rakigame.com/news/2017/10/29/the-american-academy-of-pediatrics-interviewed-sara-hope-about-our-random-app-of-kindness-empathy-app-check-it-out.

"More or Less Human." *Radiolab*, May 17, 2018. https://www.wnyc-studios.org/story/more-or-less-human.

Morris, Robert R., Kareem Kouddous, Rohan Kshirsagar, and Stephen M. Schueller. "Towards an Artificially Empathic Conversational Agent for Mental Health Applications: System Design and User Perceptions." *Journal of Medical Internet Research* 20, no. 6 (June 2018). https://www.jmir.org/2018/6/e10148.

Moye, David. "Sex Robot Molested at Electronics Festival, Creators Say." HuffPost, September 29, 2017. https://www.huffpost.com/entry/samantha-sex-robot-molested_n_59cec9f9e4b06791bb10a268.

Mozur, Paul. "A Genocide Incited on Facebook, with Posts from Myanmar's Military." *New York Times*, October 15, 2018. https://www.nytimes.com/2018/10/15/technology/myanmar-facebook-genocide.html.

National Center for Chronic Disease Prevention and Health Promotion. "Screen Time vs. Lean Time Infographic." Centers for Disease Control and Prevention, last modified March 13, 2017. https://www.cdc.gov/nccdphp/dch/multimedia/infographics/getmoving.htm.

NBCNews.com. "MSNBC.com Wins National Press Club 'Best Journalism Site' Award for the Fourth Time." Press release, June 12, 2006. http://www.nbcnews.com/id/14245195/ns/about-press_releases/t/msnbccom-wins-national-press-club-best-journalism-site-award-fourth-time.

NBCNews.com. "Rising from Ruin: Two Towns Rebuild After Katrina." Press release, October 20, 2005. http://www.nbcnews.com/id/9898349/t/press-release.

Neumann, Melanie, Friedrich Edelhäuser, Diethard Tauschel, Martin R. Fischer, Markus Wirtz, Christiane Woopen, Aviad Haramati, and Christian Scheffer. "Empathy Decline and Its Reasons: A Systematic Review of Studies with Medical Students and Residents." *Academic Medicine* 86, no. 8 (August 2011): 996–1009. https://www.ncbi.nlm.nih.gov/pubmed/21670661.

Newton, Katy, and Karin Soukup. "The Storyteller's Guide to the Virtual Reality Audience." Medium, April 6, 2016. https://medium.com/stanford-d-school/the-storyteller-s-guide-to-the-virtual-reality-audience-19e92da57497.

Novacic, Ines. "How Might Virtual Reality Change the World? Stanford Lab Peers into Future." *CBS News*, June 28, 2015. https://www.cbsnews.com/news/how-might-virtual-reality-change-the-world-stanford-lab-peers-into-future.

O'Neil, Cathy. "Enter the Holodeck." *New York Times Book Review*, January 30, 2018. https://www.nytimes.com/2018/01/30/books/review/virtual-reality-jaron-lanier-jeremy-bailenson.html.

O'Neil, Cathy. "The Ivory Tower Can't Keep Ignoring Tech." *New York Times*, November 14, 2017. https://www.nytimes.com/2017/11/14/opinion/academia-tech-algorithms.html.

Olson, Parmy. "Exclusive: WhatsApp Cofounder Brian Acton Gives the Inside Story on #DeleteFacebook and Why He Left $850 Million Behind." *Forbes*, September 26, 2018. https://www.forbes.

com/sites/parmyolson/2018/09/26/exclusive-whatsapp-cofounder-brian-acton-gives-the-inside-story-on-deletefacebook-and-why-he-left-850-million-behind.

Perspective. Website for Perspective API, accessed May 22, 2019. https://www.perspectiveapi.com.

Pinger, Laura, and Lisa Flook. "What If Schools Taught Kindness?" Greater Good Magazine (online), February 1, 2016. https://greatergood.berkeley.edu/article/item/what_if_schools_taught_kindness.

Planned Parenthood. "Across the Line Evaluation Overview." https://www.plannedparenthood.org/uploads/filer_public/4a/5c/4a5c911e-44a5-4937-b8d9-f7b1cb821112/atlexec-summary.pdf.

Re:Work. "Learn about Google's Workshop Experiment." Google re:Work, accessed May 22, 2019. https://rework.withgoogle.com/guides/unbiasing-raise-awareness/steps/learn-about-Googles-workshop-experiment.

Robb, Michael. "Kids' Screen Time Shifts Dramatically toward Phones and Tablets." Common Sense Media, October 18, 2017. https://www.commonsensemedia.org/blog/kids-screen-time-shifts-dramatically-toward-phones-and-tablets.

Robertson, Adi. "You Can Download the *New York Times*' Virtual Reality Journalism App Today." The Verge, November 5, 2015. https://www.theverge.com/2015/11/5/9676840/nyt-vr-google-cardboard-app-the-displaced-released.

Rosenthal-von der Pütten, Astrid M., Frank P. Schulte, Sabrina C. Eimler, Sabrina Sobieraj, Laura Hoffmann, Stefan Maderwald, Matthias Brand, and Nicole C. Krämer. "Investigations on Empathy towards Humans and Robots Using fMRI." *Computers in Human Behavior* 33 (April 2014): 201–12. https://doi.org/10.1016/j.chb.2014.01.004.

Rosenthal-von der Pütten, Astrid Marieke, Nicole Krämer, Laura Hoffmann, Sabrina Sobieraj, and Sabrina Eimler. "An Experimental Study on Emotional Reactions towards a Robot." *International Journal of Social Robotics* 5, no. 1 (November 2013): 17–34. http://doi.org/10.1007/s12369-012-0173-8.

Sakuma, Amanda. "Facebook Reportedly Used Anti-Semitic Attacks to Discredit Its Critics." Vox, November 14, 2018. https://www.vox.com/2018/11/14/18096008/facebook-zuckerberg-data-crisis-denial-antisemitism.

Salmanowitz, Natalie. "Thync Piece: Do Mind-Altering Wearables Live Up to the Billing?" *New Scientist*, April 5, 2016. https://www.newscientist.com/article/2083126-thync-piece-do-mind-altering-wearables-live-up-to-the-billing.

Sampasa-Kanyinga, Hugues, and Rosamund F. Lewis. "Frequent Use of Social Networking Sites Is Associated with Poor Psychological Functioning among Children and Adolescents." *Cyberpsychology, Behavior, and Social Networking* 18, no. 7 (2015): 380–5. http://doi.org/10.1089/cyber.2015.0055.

Sanders, Robert. "Sprinkling of Neural Dust Opens Door to Electroceuticals." Berkeley News, August 3, 2016. https://

news.berkeley.edu/2016/08/03/sprinkling-of-neural-dust-opens-door-to-electroceuticals.

Schouela, Adam. "Applying Virtual Reality for Empathy Training." Fidelity Labs blog, April 09, 2019. https://www.fidelitylabs. com/2019/04/09/applying-virtual-reality-for-empathy-training.

Schroeder, Juliana, Michael Kardas, and Nicholas Epley. "The Humanizing Voice: Speech Reveals, and Text Conceals, a More Thoughtful Mind in the Midst of Disagreement." *Psychological Science* 28, no. 12 (December 2017): 1745–62. http://faculty.haas. berkeley.edu/jschroeder/Publications/SchroederKardasEpley%20 Humanizing%20Voice%20Psych%20Science.pdf.

Segovia, Kathryn Y., and Jeremy N. Bailenson. "Virtually True: Children's Acquisition of False Memories in Virtual Reality." *Media Psychology* 12, no. 4 (2009): 371–93. https://vhil.stanford.edu/ mm/2009/segovia-virtually-true.pdf.

Shakya, Holly B., and Nicholas A. Christakis. "Association of Facebook Use with Compromised Well-Being: A Longitudinal Study." *American Journal of Epidemiology* 185, no. 3 (February 2017): 203–11. https://doi.org/10.1093/aje/kww189.

Shankland, Stephen. "Facebook Starts Building AI with an Ethical Compass." CNET, May 2, 2018. https://www.cnet.com/news/ facebook-starts-building-ai-with-an-ethical-compass.

Shead, Sam. "Facebook Backs University AI Ethics Institute with $7.5 Million." *Forbes*, January 20, 2019. https:// www.forbes.com/sites/samshead/2019/01/20/facebook-backs-university-ai-ethics-institute-with-7-5-million/amp.

Shiozawa, Pedro, Mailu Enokibara da Silva, Geraldo Teles Machado Netto, Ivan Taiar, and Quirino Cordeiro. "Effect of a 10-Day Trigeminal Nerve Stimulation (TNS) Protocol for Treating Major Depressive Disorder: A Phase II, Sham-Controlled, Randomized Clinical Trial." *Epilepsy & Behavior* 44 (March 1, 2015): 23–26. https://www.ncbi.nlm.nih.gov/pubmed/25597529.

Sinclair, Kamal. "In Summary: Making a New Reality." Making A New Reality, August 27, 2018. https://makinganewreality.org/making-a-new-reality-summary-3fc8741595ef.

Skitka, Linda J., Christopher W. Bauman, and Edward G. Sargis. "Moral Conviction: Another Contributor to Attitude Strength or Something More?" *Journal of Personality and Social Psychology* 88, no. 6 (2005): 895–917. https://lskitka.people.uic.edu/MCs.pdf.

Somashekhar, Sandhya. "The Disturbing Reason Some African American Patients May Be Undertreated for Pain." *Washington Post*, April 4, 2016. https://www.washington-post.com/news/to-your-health/wp/2016/04/04/do-blacks-feel-less-pain-than-whites-their-doctors-may-think-so.

Sparrow, Robert. "The March of the Robot Dogs." *Ethics and Information Technology* 4, no. 4 (December 2002): 305–18. https://www.cs.cmu.edu/~social/reading/Sparrow1.pdf.

Stewart, Emily. "Facebook Agrees to Civil Rights Audit Update, Apologizes for Soros Opposition Research." Vox, November 30, 2018. https://www.vox.com/policy-and-politics/2018/11/27/18113343/facebook-color-of-change-meeting-george-soros.

Swisher, Kara. "Mark Zuckerberg Clarifies: 'I Personally Find Holocaust Denial Deeply Offensive, and I Absolutely Didn't Intend to Defend the Intent of People Who Deny That.'" Vox, Jul 18, 2018. https://www.vox.com/2018/7/18/17588116/mark-zuckerberg-clarifies-holocaust-denial-offensive.

Swisher, Kara. "The Expensive Education of Mark Zuckerberg and Silicon Valley." New York Times, August 2, 2018. https://www.nytimes.com/2018/08/02/opinion/the-expensive-education-of-mark-zuckerberg-and-silicon-valley.html.

Swoboda, Dave, Marcus Thiebaux, Rita Addison, and David Zeltzer. Detour: Brain Deconstruction Area Ahead. VR experience. Electronic Visualization Laboratory, July 15, 1994. https://www.evl.uic.edu/entry.php?id=1724.

Szirniks, Taimaz. "Fake News: Algorithms in the Dock." Phys.org, July 14, 2018. https://phys.org/news/2018-07-fake-news-algorithms-dock.html.

The Nielsen Company. "2016 Nielsen Social Media Report." 2017. https://www.nielsen.com/us/en/insights/report/2017/2016-nielsen-social-media-report.

The Nielsen Company. "Time Flies: US Adults Now Spend Nearly Half a Day Interacting with Media." Nielsen.com, July 31, 2018. https://www.nielsen.com/us/en/insights/article/2018/time-flies-us-adults-now-spend-nearly-half-a-day-interacting-with-media.

The Travelers Companies. "Travelers Partners with Cedars-Sinai, Samsung Electronics America, Bayer and AppliedVR to Test Digital

Tools in Treatment of Acute Orthopaedic Injuries." Press release. Business Wire, March 6, 2018. https://www.businesswire.com/news/home/20180306006190/en/Travelers-Partners-Cedars-Sinai-Samsung-Electronics-America-Bayer.

Torres, Nicole. "Research: Technology Is Only Making Social Skills More Important." *Harvard Business Review*, August 26, 2015. https://hbr.org/2015/08/research-technology-is-only-making-social-skills-more-important.

Tulsky, James A., Robert M. Arnold, Stewart C. Alexander, Maren K. Olsen, Amy S. Jeffreys, Keri L. Rodriguez, Celette Sugg Skinner, David Farrell, Amy P. Abernethy, and Kathryn I. Pollak. "Enhancing Communication between Oncologists and Patients with a Computer-Based Training Program: A Randomized Trial." *Annals of Internal Medicine* 155, no. 9 (November 1, 2011): 593–601. https://www.ncbi.nlm.nih.gov/pubmed/22041948.

Twenge, Jean M. "Have Smartphones Destroyed a Generation?" *Atlantic*, September 2017. https://www.theatlantic.com/magazine/archive/2017/09/has-the-smartphone-destroyed-a-generation/534198.

Ugolik, Kaitlin. "Can an Algorithm Solve Comment Section Trolling?" *Columbia Journalism Review*, August 13, 2014. https://archives.cjr.org/behind_the_news/comment_moderation_algorithm.php.

Ugolik, Kaitlin. "Can Virtual Reality Change Minds on Social Issues?" Narratively, November 1, 2017. https://narratively.com/can-virtual-reality-change-minds-social-issues.

Ugolik, Kaitlin. "The Future of Empathy-Building Tech." Establishment, February 4, 2017. https://medium.com/the-establishment/the-future-of-empathy-building-tech-df6426ccd2cb.

University of Huddersfield News. "Doctors Gain a Greater Understanding of Skin Cancer Using Tattoos." University of Huddersfield, September 2017. https://www.hud.ac.uk/news/2017/september/doctorsgainagreaterunderstandingofskincancerusingtattoos.

Vincent, James. "Google 'Fixed' Its Racist Algorithm by Removing Gorillas from Its Image-Labeling Tech." Verge, January 12, 2018. https://www.theverge.com/2018/1/12/16882408/google-racist-gorillas-photo-recognition-algorithm-ai.

Virtual Reality Society. "Who Coined the Term 'Virtual Reality'?" Website of the Virtual Reality Society, accessed May 22, 2019. https://www.vrs.org.uk/virtual-reality/who-coined-the-term.html.

Virtual Relief. Website of Virtual Relief organization, accessed May 22, 2019. http://virtualrelief.org.

VitalSmarts. "New Study Shows It's Never Been Riskier to Talk about Politics." Press release, May 3, 2016. https://www.vitalsmarts.com/press/2016/05/new-study-shows-its-never-been-riskier-to-talk-about-politics.

Vossen, Helen G. M., and Patti M. Valkenburg. "Do Social Media Foster or Curtail Adolescents' Empathy? A Longitudinal Study." *Computers in Human Behavior* 63, no. C (October 2016): 118–124. https://dl.acm.org/citation.cfm?id=2988668.

Warrier, Varun, Roberto Toro, Bhismadev Chakrabarti, the iPSYCH-Broad autism group, Anders D. Børglum, Jakob Grove, the 23andMe Research Team, David A. Hinds, Thomas Bourgeron, and Simon Baron-Cohen. "Genome-Wide Analyses of Self-Reported Empathy: Correlations with Autism, Schizophrenia, and Anorexia Nervosa." *Translational Psychiatry* 8, no. 1 (2018): 35. https://doi.org/10.1038/s41398-017-0082-6.

Winkler, Rolfe, Daisuke Wakabayashi, and Elizabeth Dwoskin. "Apple Buys Artificial-Intelligence Startup Emotient." *Wall Street Journal*, January 7, 2016. https://www.wsj.com/articles/apple-buys-artificial-intelligence-startup-emotient-1452188715.

Zhang, Justine, Jonathan P. Chang, Cristian Danescu-Niculescu-Mizil, Lucas Dixon, Yiqing Hua, Nithum Thain, and Dario Taraborelli. "Conversations Gone Awry: Detecting Early Signs of Conversational Failure." *Proceedings of the 56th Annual Meeting of the Association for Computational Linguistics (Long Papers)*, Melbourne, Australia, July 15–20, 2018. https://www.aclweb.org/anthology/P18-1125.

ABOUT THE AUTHOR

Photo © 2018 Rebecca Faulk

Kaitlin Ugolik Phillips is a journalist and editor who lives in Raleigh, North Carolina. Her writing on law, finance, health, and technology has appeared in the Establishment, VICE, Quartz, *Institutional Investor* magazine, Law360, *Columbia Journalism Review*, and Narratively, among others. She writes a blog and newsletter about empathy featuring reportage, essays, and interviews. For more information, visit www.kaitlinugolik.com.